NURTURING

PEACE

HOW FAMILIES CAN HELP INCARCERATED LOVED
ONES CHANGE THEIR LIVES

Kirk Blackard

Bridges To Life Books ● Houston, Texas

also by Kirk Blackard

Restoring Peace: Using Lessons from Prison to Mend Broken Relationships

love in a cauldron of misery: perspectives on Christian prison ministry

Makin' It: A Story of Hope

Nurturing Peace

How Families Can Help Incarcerated Loved Ones Change Their Lives

© Copyright 2014 Kirk Blackard and Bridges To Life

All rights reserved. No part of this publication may be reproduced, stored in a retrieval system, or transmitted, in any form or by any means, electronic, mechanical, photocopying, recording, or otherwise, without the written prior permission of the Author or Bridges To Life.

ISBN-13: 978-1500672256

BRIDGES TO LIFE BOOKS

PRINTED IN THE UNITED STATES OF AMERICA

For information or to order additional copies, contact:

Bridges To Life
P.O. Box 19039
Houston, Texas 77224-9039
www.bridgestolife.org

Or:

www.Amazon.com

ACKNOWLEDGMENTS

A couple of years ago Tom Mechler, Vice-Chairman of the Texas Board of Criminal Justice, asked whether there is a good book that helps families work with incarcerated loved ones to avoid their returning to prison after release. John Sage, founder and Executive Director of the restorative justice program, Bridges To Life; and I considered his question. We found a number of books that addressed the "mechanics" of helping loved ones deal with the criminal justice system, but we didn't find any that focused on helping them change their lives and avoid a return. This book is intended to fill that void. Thanks to Mr. Mechler for recognizing it and providing the initial idea for *Nurturing Peace*.

The Bridges To Life program, which has been amazingly successful in helping released inmates avoid returning to prison, provided the platform. Thanks to John Sage and all the Bridges To Life volunteers for making this possible. Special thanks go to a large number of inmate volunteers who contributed directly, through interviews and written communication. They know what they need, they willingly shared their ideas, and they are much appreciated.

Thanks also to a number of family members of incarcerated individuals who willingly provided input. Their perspective was invaluable.

A number of individuals provided direct input or read and assisted with early drafts of the manuscript. Special thanks to Jan Collins, Becky Stewart, Ershell Redd, Bonnie and Doug Williams, Leslie Culver, and Danielle Sims.

CONTENTS

Acknowledgments   iv

Chapter 1: FOREWORD   1

Chapter 2: HELPING YOURSELF   7
    Accepting the Change   9
    Getting Help   11
    Establishing Goals   14

Chapter 3: CRIME AND CONFLICT   17
    Causes of Crime   18
    Addressing the Causes   24

Chapter 4: FAITH   26
    The Power of Faith   27
    Nurturing Your Loved One's Faith   32

Chapter 5: STORIES   36
    Hearing Your Loved One's Story   37
    Helping Change Your Loved One's Story   41

Chapter 6: RESPONSIBILITY   48
    Looking Back and Dealing with Consequences   48
    Looking Forward and Being Responsible   55

Chapter 7: ACCOUNTABILITY   58
    Being Accountable to Your Loved One   59
    Helping Your Loved One be Accountable   62

Chapter 8: CONFESSION	68
Being a Role Model	70
Being Present	72
Listening	73
Chapter 9: REPENTANCE	79
Understanding Empathy	80
Helping Your Loved One Develop Empathy	83
Chapter 10: FORGIVENESS	89
Forgiving Your Loved One	91
Helping Your Loved One Forgive Himself	94
Helping Your Loved One Ask for Forgiveness	95
Helping Your Loved One Forgive Others	97
Chapter 11: RECONCILIATION	101
Deciding When Reconciliation is Needed	102
Finding A Mutually Satisfying Relationship	104
Reconciling	106
Chapter 12: RESTITUTION	114
Understanding Your Loved One After Prison	116
Helping Your Loved One After Prison	118
Chapter 13: THE JOURNEY	129

1

FOREWORD

"You bridged the gap and included us in it."

An old proverb holds that "It takes a village to raise a child." This is a powerful reminder that human beings are not islands. We all need a community of loved ones to help us weather the storms of life. This is particularly true of those who have violated the law and are incarcerated for their actions. They face a storm of problems, often with little hope of rescue. They need a village—parents, spouses, siblings, extended family, friends, and others—to help them deal with their problems, straighten out their lives, and stay out of prison in the future. You are part of that village.

"Cal had no support socially, through family or friends, so Cal did his time in sort of a survival mode, there's very little hope in that mind-state."

This book addresses only one of the many difficult issues facing families of those who are incarcerated. These families (often including friends, lovers, and others) usually need help dealing with the effect on themselves of their loved one's crime. They may also need help in assisting their loved ones with the day-to-day challenges of his life; for example, dealing with the criminal justice system, handling prison issues, working on parole, and things of that sort. Neither of these concerns is the purpose of this book. Instead, this book aims to help families help incarcerated loved ones transform their lives and avoid a return to prison after their release.

But where does one even start on such an ambitious project as helping an inmate transform his or her life? I have elected to build on what works. Bridges To Life is a faith-based restorative justice program that facilitates healing for victims and offenders and helps reduce recidivism rates of prison inmates. The program requires inmates to think about their lives and face up to a number of issues, such as faith, responsibility, accountability, forgiveness, repentance and other topics. Since its inception in 2000, more than 20,000 inmates have graduated from its fourteen-week program. A study shows that they return to prison at about half the rate expected of released offenders who do not participate in a Bridges To Life program. And there is evidence that participation also brings transformation and peace into the lives of those who have not been released.

"The course taught me that I was hurting people and that I didn't have that right. I hurt people by committing crimes against them. I realized that I was violating their space with my selfishness and greed. Bridges To Life taught me how to channel my energy and become more accountable, responsible, reconcilable. I except the personal blame."

Nurturing Peace: How Families Can Help Incarcerated Loved Ones Change Their Lives builds on this very successful program. This book covers the same topics, chapter by chapter, as *Restoring Peace,* the focus of the BTL curriculum. It shows families how they can help offenders benefit from the BTL principles covered in *Restoring Peace*. Key portions of inmate correspondence are also included verbatim in a *special script.*

Ideally, family members will read *Nurturing Peace* at the same time incarcerated loved ones are participating in a Bridges To Life program or reading *Restoring Peace*. Family members can then use what they learn to encourage their incarcerated loved ones while they are in the BTL process and afterward. If working together is not possible, family members can use *Nurturing Peace* as a stand-alone guide for helping their loved ones improve their life and decrease the likelihood of another prison term.

Think carefully about what you are reading and decide what fits in your case and what does not. The book takes a "one size fits all" approach, but what you need to do will vary greatly according to circumstances. Helping a juvenile is different than helping an adult. Helping a man is different than helping a woman. (I have used the masculine gender extensively throughout the book—much more than the feminine gender—because most prison inmates are men. I believe, however, that the basic lessons apply to both.) Those dealing with a two-year sentence face different issues than those dealing with life behind bars. And on and on.

Several important themes occur time and again throughout the book. They are:

- You cannot control your loved one or force him to do anything. Even trying to do so will probably do more harm than good. All you can do is create the right environment, help, encourage, teach, and love him.
- You need to look at yourself. A family—including an extended family—is a "system." This means that every family is comprised of many related parts, and each part affects and is affected by the other parts. Just like a car, where a bad fuel injection system can prevent the entire car from running, what parents and loved ones do affects the behavior of the entire family. If you behave appropriately, your behavior positively influences your loved one's behavior. But if you behave badly, your behavior is a negative influence. Therefore, time and again this book will suggest that you look at your own behavior as an important part of helping your loved one. Simply look honestly at your life. If your behavior has been good—which is often the case—applaud yourself and move on. If you don't like what you see, don't condemn yourself. But consider the ideas presented to address your own behavior and applaud yourself when you change.

> *"Before I render another apology it's only fitting I confess my mistakes. I too didn't have the grace and peace of God demonstrated from my father. As I've talked and reasoned with elder family niether did my father. So there was a break-down that caused a cycle. That cycle consists of lack of nurturing, sacrificial-giving, and seeking the best for others."*

- Your loved one must be responsible for his own actions. Even if your behavior was a negative influence on your loved one, this does not let him off the hook or take away his responsibility for what he did. He has been and is an individual with free will. He—not you or others—made the choices and committed the crime(s). He has to deal with the aftermath. He has to straighten out his own life.

- Look to your faith for help. *Nurturing Peace* presents a Christian perspective. It contains references to the Bible, Christianity, faith and related matters, and one chapter is devoted to matters of faith. I have come to believe that faith in God is essential for inmates to become good, law-abiding citizens. And I believe biblical principles will help you help your incarcerated loved one do so. I have addressed these issues from a Christian perspective, because I am a Christian. This is not to discount other of the world's great religions.

- Listen loud. Effective listening—open and authentic sharing without criticism—tells your loved one you care and gives you information you can use in nurturing him. It underlies nearly everything you need to do to help your loved one.

- The most important help is love. 1 Corinthians 13:13 states: "And now these three remain: faith, hope and love. But the greatest of these is love."

The first five chapters are intended to provide a foundation on which you can build your efforts to help your incarcerated loved one. The second half of the book focuses on what you can do to nurture his transformation.

You can create an environment in which your loved one is more likely to make the right choices, and help him follow through on those choices. You can provide the incentive for him to develop a new sense of purpose to improve his life. You, and family and friends, can model your knowledge, experience, and love in ways that motivate him to make a better life for himself.

But all this starts with you. You need to address your own needs first if you are to help him deal with his.

THINGS TO THINK ABOUT

1. WHY ARE YOU READING THIS BOOK?

2. WHAT DO YOU HOPE TO GET FROM IT?

2

HELPING YOURSELF

"It's a program of tragedy and triumph."

Think about a flight attendant's announcement during a plane's takeoff. He instructs you in case of emergency to put your oxygen mask on first, before helping your child or another person. He understands that your top priority may be helping the other person, but without oxygen, you can't do it. This lesson also applies to family members helping imprisoned loved ones.

Having a loved one in prison probably makes you feel like a sea of tears is cutting off your life-sustaining oxygen and suffocating you. You are angry because the person was so selfish, or so mean, or so negligent, or so stupid. A person you love is being punished, perhaps severely, and you feel his or her pain. You experience a continuing sense of sadness and deep emotional trauma brought about by the uncertainty, an overwhelming sense of helpless love, and the embarrassment of admitting to family and friends that a loved one is indeed locked up for his or her misdeeds and failings. You can't explain to your four-year-old where daddy is or why he wears all white, or you get tired of telling people your son "lives in a gated community in central Texas." You hate being alone at night. Relationships with others that you thought were strong or positive are failing, as friends or family members condemn you, or perhaps more predictably and worse, ignore your pain and try to go on like nothing is happening. Your relationship with God may be suffering, as you ask why and don't get an answer you understand or accept. You have lost a bread-winner, have to be both mother and father, and can't figure out where the next meal is coming from. The cost of defending and supporting your loved one, in time and money, has put you in a hole from which you see no escape. Or the kids are rebelling and you can't handle them without your spouse. You don't know what to do next. You are losing sleep, weight, strength, concentration, judgment, faith, and peace. You may be in despair, and feel life can't get much worse.

"Baby,

Just wanted to write & tell first of all how sorry I am for leaving you & for the way it went down. I'll be back as soon as I possibly can but until then it's gonna be up to you to hold everthing together. Your gonna have to carry a dubble load on all the everday things like the bills, cookin, cleaning, taking care of the dog & the yard and the day to day crap that come up. On top of all that there are both our paren to deal with. You have to decide what & how much to tell them. Then you will have to deal with your mom putting me down & trying to constantly get you to leave me & my mom simply telling you it's all you fault & not being welcome there anymore after all these years of you trying so hard to get her to like you."

But you hope that your incarcerated loved one will believe God has a plan for him, and will use the prison experience to transform his life. There is little to suggest your loved one will do it alone. He will need your help, and you want to help him.

Like an airline passenger in an emergency, you need to help yourself first. Failing to do so will probably lead to anger, frustration, and resentment. In the end everyone will suffer. This doesn't mean you ignore her at the beginning of her incarceration, when the need for help and support is probably greatest. But it does mean that you take the long view, and start by focusing on yourself rather than on the person who is locked up. You may help your loved one less at the start than either of you would like, so you can heal and grow and in the end be able to help her more.

The purpose of this book is to help family members help loved ones who are locked up. Therefore, helping family members help themselves will largely be left to others. But I can't pass the opportunity to offer some ideas for you to think about.

ACCEPTING THE CHANGE

Change is a process where we move from where we are (our status quo), through a period of transition, to a new place, or a new status quo. Sometimes we change because we want to, and sometimes change is forced on us. Sometimes we move to a better place, and sometimes we move in the opposite direction. Most change is frightening. It usually involves a period of major uncertainty where we just don't know what we will have to deal with or what will happen to us.

Think of some changes you have experienced: Moving from a comfortable school to one that is new and different. Moving to a new house or new town. Starting a new job. Getting married. Getting divorced. Having children. A loved one dies. And think of a time when you knew your life was changing, when you couldn't turn back but you also couldn't see the road ahead very well. Scary, wasn't it? Letting go of what you know and are comfortable with, and losing the order and predictability of your life, is scary, often painful, even when the change is something we want or have prayed for.

Fear of change breeds resistance and can prevent you from doing what you need to do to heal, grow, and improve your life. Think of the people who are in a bad or even abusive relationship, know they need to move on, but refuse to do so. They refuse to move on because they fear the uncertainty of change more than they object to the troubles or abuse they are currently enduring.

When a loved one is locked up, everyone involved experiences change. The inmate moves from a state of freedom to a state of incarceration. This causes major change on you and your family. Your relationships with friends are now different. You now have to be the primary breadwinner. The kids get teased at school and start behaving badly. You have to move in with your parents.

You need to make frequent long drives for visits. Or you make the difficult decision to refrain from visits for personal or economic reasons and cause additional strife with your incarcerated loved one. You have a fundamentally new and different life.

> *"I'm killing our mother. I've been to prison 3 times and each time seems more worse than the last. My mother doesn't think she'll live to see me free and it's her fear."*

Thus, your life changes when a loved one is incarcerated. How do you deal with what is happening to you? Start with an effort at "mental adjustment" in five areas.

- Recognize the stability that remains in your life: Your love among family members, the friends that stand by you, your faith in God, and many others. Remember, "Jesus Christ is the same yesterday and today and forever." (Hebrews 13:8)
- Acknowledge that your life will probably never be the same again, and more change is coming. Don't try to run and hide. Talk to people who love you about your changed situation. Write in a journal about it. Talk to or write to your incarcerated loved one about it—not to blame him, rag on him, or keep on reliving the past—but to help you deal with it and begin to lay the groundwork for helping him accept responsibility for the consequences of his actions.

> *"I'm telling you these things because I didn't let you know from the git-go what you were getting into & that was wrong & you deserve better. At least this way I know that win, lose, or draw, I shot strait with you. Just know that whatever I love you & always will."*

- Change how you think about change. Remember that change is a process and not an event. It's not a one-time action like turning a light on and off. Instead, change is like baking bread, involving several ingredients and a series of actions performed over time. Since it involves a series of events over time, you can be in charge. Your choices determine the result. This starts with your thoughts and attitudes about what has happened. Negative thoughts block your creativity and ability to solve problems. Positive thoughts create opportunities. View your cup as half full rather than half empty.

- Honestly face your feelings about what has happened. Any feeling is okay, but many need to be dealt with and put behind you. For example, get past the feeling of "Why me?" or "This isn't fair." Don't see yourself as a victim of your loved one's behavior. Don't be ashamed of what has happened. Other good people have been through this experience, too. Be willing to consider that there may be something positive in what has happened.
- Look to the future, and think about changes you need to foster. Identify those things about your life that are okay and need to stay the same, and those areas where you need more change. Think about what changes you need to make in order to help your loved one with the dramatic changes he needs to face to transform his life.

Changing the way you think and feel about what is happening to you is just the start. You will also face more immediate problems, such as dealing with misbehaving kids, or finding a higher paying job, or buying a car that works. None of these is easy, and they rarely can be accomplished alone. You will need help.

GETTING HELP

In many ways you and your incarcerated loved one probably are much alike. Both of your lives are in turmoil, and you cannot effectively deal with them alone. You both need help.

You may believe that seeking help undermines your independence and questions your ability to cope, or will be seen as a sign of weakness, or will leave you somehow obligated when you want to be free. You may be afraid of rejection or reluctant to burden another person with your problems. Or you realize asking for help means you might have to admit to your situation when you were trying to keep it "in the family."

Don't try to be a hero and do it on your own! Heroes and people of great accomplishment nearly always have many others supporting them. Think of the successful corporate executive with thousands of people behind her, or the hero quarterback with an entire team blocking and tackling for him. All need help.

Asking for and accepting help involves some ideas that seem contrary to common sense. Thinking about them will help you deal with your reluctance to ask for help.

- Asking for and accepting help is a sign of strength, not weakness. The weak approach is to bury your problems, run, and hide. The strong approach is to face up to them, be open about them, and ask for and accept help. Be strong, and ask.
- Trust so others will trust you. To receive help, trust yourself and others—that you are worthy of help and can make the most of it, and that others will act in good faith. You will probably have to take the risk of asking for and accepting help before you know what the result will be. But when the results are good, this will build trust and make it easier the next time.
- Deal with your fear of rejection by opening yourself up and allowing others to judge, and perhaps reject, you. They rarely will, and when they come through, your fear will go away.
- Give in order to help yourself and receive help. Giving involves sharing your skills, talents, and abilities with those who also are in need of help. Giving to others helps them learn more about you and your commitment to make things work, and a reciprocal relationship (You scratch my back,

I'll scratch yours.) to develop. When you stop focusing on yourself, it becomes easier for you to accept help from others.

In summary, if a loved one is incarcerated you will probably need to ask for help. This leads us to the second problem, which involves deciding where to go for help. Consider seeking help from each of three sources.

- Look first to God. Faith in God will be discussed in more detail in Chapter 4, but for now consider two ideas: First, approach matters of faith very personally, privately. Read the Bible regularly, and supplement it with other good, spiritually relevant books. Pray regularly, give thanks for your many blessings (and you have many) and ask for God's help with your problems. And second, join a religious community. Doing so will help you learn more about God and how to approach him with your needs. A religious community will, in nearly all cases, be a helping, healing community. If you need help, a church community will offer it.
- Get help from your family and friends. You may be embarrassed to admit that a loved one is locked up, and relationships with friends or family members may be failing because of the incarceration. But they know you and your needs better than others, and they have the greatest incentive to help you. If they have been ignoring your situation or condemning you, they probably don't have all the facts. They need to be educated and made comfortable. If you ask for help, even if you cannot define anything specific, you will probably find those closest to you will be relieved you did so. Talk to them, tell them about your life, and explain how they can help—which may vary from "just be my friend and listen to me" to requests for more specific assistance such as "help me get a car so I can get to work."

They will most likely be quite helpful in suggesting ways they can help in areas they feel they are equipped to do so.
- Contact organized groups of like-minded people. Some, such as the Texas Inmate Families Association, are comprised of people who are where you are and are committed to strengthening families of incarcerated members through direct support, education, and advocacy. Other groups, such as Kairos or Bridges To Life, aim primarily to help inmates themselves or victims of crime. Many churches support or are involved with prison ministries. The internet is replete with opportunities. While all are different, many bring together people who have some understanding of the difficulties associated with prison and a desire to help. Pick some that look good, and check them out.

ESTABLISHING GOALS

Nearly all successful people set goals—top-level athletes, successful business-people, and achievers in all fields. Thoughtful goals give you a vision of where you want to be in the future and the motivation to achieve. They also help you set priorities, organize your time and resources, and measure the results.

Goals may be long-term or even life-time plans that shape many aspects of our shorter-term decision making. But long-term plans can come later. Now you need to get through this difficult time. You need goals to help you handle today's problems.

This is not the place for an extensive discussion of goals. Information is readily available in other books and on the internet. Briefly, however, your goals should identify specific things you plan to accomplish, with specific action steps and time lines for accomplishing them. The plans need to be organized and written. They also need to be measurable, certainly to the extent that you will know when you are on track and when your goals are accomplished. The following should help you get started.

- Decide on the time frame you are dealing with. If your loved one is incarcerated for a short term, plan for the time you anticipate she will be locked up. If she will be gone for many years, you may wish to set a planning term that aims to get you over the initial hump and make your life manageable over the long term.
- Think about your life as it is, changes you need to make, and the biggest problems to be solved. Consider many possible issues, such as financial, family issues, spiritual issues, transportation, living situation, education, marital status, social life, and on and on. Select the three to five concerns that are most pressing. Write down the things that need to be different for each of the important issues. These are your goals.
- For each of your goals, identify several short-term tasks to accomplish along the way, and when you need to accomplish them to reach your final goal.
- Monitor your goals on a frequent basis—at least monthly, perhaps more often. Be sure you are accomplishing your identified short-term tasks and are making progress. When your highest priority goals have been accomplished, move to others.

Follow-up on your goals is critical. If you are not making progress, decide why and correct your course. When you accomplish a goal, reward yourself, mark it off, and move on to the next issue on your list of priorities. Establish a new, specific, written goal with a time target. And then start to work on it.

You now understand that you probably should help yourself before you try to help your loved one. It's time to move on to him or her. Let's first lay the groundwork by considering the broad subject of crime, and the reasons for most criminal behavior.

THINGS TO THINK ABOUT

1. MY LIFE HAS CHANGED IN THE FOLLOWING WAYS BECAUSE OF _____ BEING IN PRISON:

2. MY BIGGEST CHALLENGES IN DEALING WITH THESE CHANGES ARE:

    a. FINANCIAL—
    b. TRANSPORTATION—
    c. SOCIAL—
    d. SPIRITUAL—
    e. PLEASURE—
    f. HOUSING—
    g. RELATIONSHIPS—
    h. CHILDREN—
    i. EDUCATION—
    j. OTHER—

3. MY SPECIFIC, MEASURABLE GOALS FOR DEALING WITH THE THREE MOST IMPORTANT CHALLENGES ARE:

4. MY BEST SOURCES OF HELP ARE:

3
CRIME AND CONFLICT

"I thought the only one I hurt was myself, but now I know there were others."

On July 25, 2000, a Concorde Supersonic jet crashed on take-off near Paris, France, killing all 109 people onboard. Investigators seeking to prevent recurrence of similar incidents reached the following [greatly simplified] conclusions: Flames were shooting from its left wing as it lifted off the runway, and it crashed shortly thereafter. Fuel leaked from a fuel tank and ignited. A tire disintegrated during takeoff and a piece of the tire struck the fuel tank, causing a rupture. A piece of debris on the runway cut the tire and began a chain of events that led to the explosion.

To prevent other Concordes from crashing officials had to know more. They had to get to the bottom of the situation, see what was not obvious, and understand that there were many contributing factors, including something as basic as debris on the runway.

Similarly, to help a loved one who has flamed out and crashed in prison you need to consider more than what is on the surface. You need to understand the more fundamental cause or causes—often called the "root cause"—of his crime or crimes. A root cause of a crime is the seed: the most basic, not the most obvious, cause of the crime—like the debris on the runway. This seed often starts to grow in a pattern of inappropriate behavior that occurred prior to the actual criminal activity.

The simplest definition of crime is "behavior that violates the law." Our laws generally reflect the moral sense of our community, and tell us what is right and wrong as well as what the government has outlawed. Your loved one no doubt broke one or several of those laws and is suffering the consequences.

Experts often do not agree as to why people disobey rules, hurt other people, or commit crimes. However, studies show that at its most basic level, crime is primarily the result of three complex and interrelated influences: economic factors and poverty, social environment, and family structure.

Unfortunately, there's not much an offender can do about these influences of his past. Hoping for a better past does him no good. But he can deal with his current beliefs and behavior patterns that are the basic causes of his specific criminal acts. Thus, his starting point, and yours if you are to help him help himself, is to think deeply about his beliefs and behavior that are the root cause of his crime. This will allow you to begin to change at the basic level.

CAUSES OF CRIME

Certain types of behavior tend to be important underlying causes of most of the problems for which people are incarcerated. And there is rarely just one cause. Usually several work together, and perhaps build on one another. These behavior patterns are discussed very briefly below. Understanding those that seem to have affected your loved one will help you help him. Like sweeping the runway to remove the debris, he needs to address them to prevent a future crash.

Different Perspectives

Our perspective is what we believe and how we see the world in which we live. Our perspective is determined by many influences—such as the lessons we learned from our parents, the way people around us live, our experiences and education, our culture and the way the media reflects it, the way our brains process information, our own self-concept and expectations.

"I am not going to pretend that I did not understand what I did was wrong. What I will say is, The social environment I grew up in was okay to commit a crime. It was even looked at as a badge of honor. Even though I saw and done things that no child should have to see or do. I

do understand how my background has shaped how I seen the world."

Because people have different perspectives, they often make different decisions as to what is right and wrong in a particular situation. A kid who has had to "hustle" all his life has few reservations about dealing drugs or stealing from Wal-Mart because he doesn't see that he is hurting anyone. His views are different from the people who make the laws and the police who enforce them.

Thus, a basic cause of much criminal activity is that the offender's perspective is different than society's. He does not distinguish between right and wrong the same way society does. He sees nothing wrong with dealing drugs, or taking what he needs, or other offenses, so he does them, gets caught, and is sent to prison. Your loved one may see nothing wrong with the behavior that led to his incarceration. If so, he is likely to repeat it.

Confusing Needs and Wants

Needs are what we can't do without: adequate food and clothing, a roof over our head, reasonable transportation, and other items necessary for our physical livelihood. We also need those things necessary for our spiritual life as well as our psychological requirements such as love and self-esteem.

Wants are what we desire because we like them or they make us feel better, but they are not essential to our well-being.

"I believed in doing what I wanted to do."

In America most people can get what they need without violating the law. Difficult as it may be, most people can legally fulfill their basic needs, even if sometimes they have to swallow their pride and accept help when they don't really want to.

Many needs exist because people satisfy their wants first. Think of the female offender who says she forged checks and engaged in shoplifting because she needed money to pay the rent and feed her children. But her wants were the reason she was short on money. She spent too much time in bars, bought too many cigarettes, drove a car she couldn't afford, and partied so much she lost her job.

Uncontrolled want can cause people to do things that violate the law. Think of the woman who shoplifted because she wanted a new blouse to make her feel better, or the teenager who stole a car because he thought he needed a more powerful one to impress his friends. Uncontrolled wants led to behavior that was a direct violation of the law—and led each of them to prison. Unless they learn to do without, or defer, things they want but don't need, they are likely to return to prison after they are released.

Abuse of Power and Control

Sometimes people feel a need to exercise power over and control other people. And sometimes they impose their power and control through violence. This is particularly true in the case of domestic abuse—involving actual or threatened physical harm, intimidation, name-calling, put-downs, unreasonable withholding of money, public or private ridicule and humiliation, continual criticism, and other harmful behavior; and sexual assault in its many egregious forms. These types of offenses typically are not about meeting legitimate needs, taking care of a family, or even sex. They usually are about power and control, and the abuse of both.

"Having to explain to a homicide detective how one of your ex-boyfriends had grabbed you as you walked home from work one late night, tied you up and cut off your hair. It was a lot for me as a nine year old to translate and today I'm left with a lot of questions that I don't expect for you to answer, but I do want you to know how that and more has impacted me, both growing up an as an adult."

Those who try to control others through violence are likely to have deeper issues, and one can reasonably predict that perpetrators of domestic violence and sexual assault have observed or experienced such offenses themselves. People who were supposed to love them abused them instead, and they abuse those they are supposed to love. From generation to generation, the sins of the parents are passed to the children and others. Unless there is effective intervention, all are likely to commit more similar offenses.

If a spouse or other family member has allowed need for power and control to lead to crime, addressing the crime itself likely will be of little value. To help the perpetrator, one needs to offer more fundamental assistance, such as helping him deal with his own history, understand why he is doing what he is doing, and develop compassion and empathy for his victims.

Confusing Respect with Fear or Envy

A man is beaten to death by two friends because he failed to pay for their meal as he had promised. One guy fails to pay a five dollar gambling debt, and the other stabs him. A young man shoots another because he gave him some lip. Why do people become violent over such small things?

Some people say it all boils down to a question of respect. The offender wants to be "respected," and may fight, steal, sell drugs, join a gang, or do whatever else is needed to gain that respect. But the more likely case is that the offender wants others to fear him for what he might do or envy him for what he has.

Using fear to impose one's will on another fosters conflict, fights, and criminal behavior. A person who is envious and wants what another has, or wants to be seen as another is seen, often does what is necessary to get what he wants, also resulting in conflict, fights, and criminal behavior.

One earns respect by being an honorable human being—not by striking fear in others or taking advantage of their envy. Earned respect leads to self-respect, often defined as a sense of worth or as due respect for one's self. It is the opposite of shame, putting one's self down, arrogance, and self-importance. Helping your loved one learn to respect others and himself will help him avoid the use of fear and envy, and the resulting conflict and crime.

Uncontrolled Anger

Feeling anger is okay, sometimes even helpful. It often tells us when we have issues we need to address, and motivates us to fix bad situations and make changes that will improve our lives and relationships. If we have a healthy approach to anger, we do what we can to address its cause and get on with our life.

"For years I was mad about that truth, at you and I still feel ashamed to admit it. I became rebellious and focused my anger on the kids I had fights with in school when they'd come trying me and I won't lie to you mom it became such a pattern that I'd even begin in aggression and start fights myself."

Uncontrolled, continuing anger is different. It can be the first step toward violent behavior. Anger can easily become a bigger and bigger problem when one person responds to another person's behavior, perhaps with an even stronger action. Anger is met with anger, threats are met with threats, and violence is met with violence. Unless one person breaks the sequence, conflict grows through cycles of increasingly serious behavior. And for many people, the ultimate consequence of the escalating cycle of anger is crime and prison.

Substance Abuse and Addiction

"When I turned 15 years old, I had ran away from home so many times, my parents wouldn't even give me any money anymore because they knew that I would just go buy drugs with it."

Offenders are incarcerated for many reasons, ranging from shoplifting to murder. A huge proportion—one study showed 80 percent—of offenders were motivated or affected by alcohol, illegal drugs, or both during the time of their offense. People commit crimes to support their habits. Drugs make people too sensitive, impair their judgment, and confuse their view of reality. They make them try to manipulate and control people. They make them feel shame—and uncontrolled anger. They often lead people to prison. If the addiction is not dealt with, those people are likely to keep returning to prison.

"I now realize that through my drug use that I had a non-caring attitude towards society and the many people whom I have hurt."

Mental Disability

A recent study indicated that more than half of all prison and jail inmates had a mental health problem of some type. Schizophrenia, bipolar disorder, post-traumatic stress disorder, depression, severe personality disorders, traumatic brain injury, and addictive disorders are overrepresented in the prison population. The severity of these illnesses varies significantly. But they often lead to crime.

Our prison system often serves as a warehouse for the mentally ill, many of whom are locked up for relatively minor offenses. By relying on extremely restrictive housing for mentally ill inmates and marginally effective mental health practices, prisons often act as incubators for worse illness and psychiatric breakdowns. Without help, offenders with mental health problems are likely to go in and out of the revolving prison doors.

"In prison there is no medical help for mental issues, but because I'm tired of hurting I decided that it was time to let God and Jesus really become part of my life

and learn to trust in them to help me. I'm dying inside and only God can save me."

ADDRESSING THE CAUSES

Your loved one is not likely to do better over the long term unless he addresses the root cause(s) of his criminal activity, such as those discussed above. Any help you give him needs to address the basic cause(s). How do you help him make better decisions if he continues to abuse drugs or is always depressed? Quit being violent if his anger persists? Stop the domestic abuse if he has never confronted the fact that he was abused?

As you read the remaining chapters of this book, think about the causes of your loved one's crimes. Help him address these basic causes. In many cases, special programs, such as abuse intervention, anger management programs, substance abuse treatment, and mental health care are available, both in prison and in the free world. Encourage your loved one to use these if they are available.

If such programs are not available, you can still focus on the causes of his offenses as you relate to him on a continuing basis. Chapter 4 suggests you rely heavily on your faith as a foundation for doing so.

THINGS TO THINK ABOUT

1. _____'S CRIME OF RECORD IS _____.

2. BASED ON WHAT I KNOW ABOUT _____, I BELIEVE THE BEHAVIOR CHECKED BELOW PROBABLY WAS AN UNDERLYING FACTOR THAT LED TO HIS CRIME:
   ___ DIFFERENT PERSPECTIVE: CONFUSING RIGHT AND WRONG
   ___ CONFUSING NEEDS AND WANTS
   ___ ABUSING POWER AND CONTROL
   ___ CONFUSING RESPECT WITH FEAR AND ENVY
   ___ UNCONTROLLED ANGER
   ___ SUBSTANCE ABUSE OR ADDICTION
   ___ MENTAL DISABILITY
   ___ OTHER?

3. I SHOULD ENCOURAGE _____ TO GET THE FOLLOWING SPECIAL HELP TO DEAL WITH THE CAUSE OR CAUSES OF HIS CRIME THAT I CHECKED ABOVE.

4. I CAN ALSO DO THE FOLLOWING TO HELP HIM DEAL WITH THE UNDERLYING CAUSE(S) OF HIS CRIMINAL ACTIVITY.

4

FAITH

"First, I want to give all the glory to God."

The Hebrews, descendants of Abraham, were Pharaoh's slaves. They groaned beneath their burdens and wept bitterly before God, but the more they were beat down, the more they seemed to multiply. God recognized their burdens and decided to deliver them from slavery to a land "flowing with milk and honey." He selected Moses to lead them from their slavery.

When the Hebrews started their trek out of Egypt, Pharaoh's army chased after them with 600 chariots. The Hebrews were frightened, cried out to God for help, and began blaming Moses for their situation. Moses told the people that everything would be okay. They should just stand and watch, as "The Lord will fight for you, and you won't need to lift a finger." But the Lord said to Moses, "Quit praying and get the people moving!" God then opened a path through the Red Sea and the people of Israel walked through to the other side. The Egyptians behind them were drowned by the returning water.

This story from Exodus provides a model for dealing with your own problems and helping your loved one. The people of Israel were required to do their part—God told Moses to quit praying and get the people moving—but they also needed God to open the sea and provide a path. Similarly, your loved one and you need to do your part to improve your situations, but you also need God's help.

Your life will not be easy. Your faith will be tested. According to 1 Peter 1: 6-7: "In all this you greatly rejoice, though now for a little while you may have had to suffer grief in all kinds of trials. These have come so that the proven genuineness of your faith—of greater worth than gold, which perishes even though refined by fire—may result in praise, glory and honor when Jesus Christ is revealed."

God has promised to care for you in times of plenty and trial. But what do you need from God? You probably need God's help and assistance in dealing with your own personal problems. You also want God to be with your loved one: provide a safe and peaceful life while she is incarcerated and transform her life for the future. Fortunately, belief in God will help both you and your loved one in several ways.

THE POWER OF FAITH

Hebrews 11: 32-34 tells of biblical characters who through faith improved their lives: "And what more shall I say? I do not have time to tell about Gideon, Barak, Samson and Jephthah, about David and Samuel and the prophets, who through faith conquered kingdoms, administered justice, and gained what was promised;…"

These individuals' faith guided them and helped them act in the present, persist, and persevere. The power of faith can do the same for you and your loved one. It can work in four important ways: belief in God lays down a great moral code that sets the standard for each of your lives; it offers hope for attaining the life that each of you wants; it demonstrates the total, never ending love that each of you need to give and receive; and it offers a process for changing to a better life. Each of these will be discussed below.

A Great Moral Code

You are in your current situation because your loved one violated the law. You may have made bad decisions in the past, as well. Regardless of the past, you and your loved one will need a strong moral compass going forward. Each of you will be facing tough decisions on many issues. Your incarcerated loved one needs to change his behavior, mend relationships with his victims, his family, and society, and transform his heart and life.

"One thing that I've learned, and its something so simple but I just never stopped to look at it that way is, God is in control of everything and he owns everything and everybody. And every time that we steal from someone or hurt someone, ware doing that directly to God ..."

Believing in God and aiming to do His will offers a practical moral compass that will guide you. The Bible establishes standards of right and wrong, provides a goal for each of you to shoot for, and guides you in getting there. Three great Bible codes will help you:

- The Ten Commandments: God promised the descendants of Abraham that He would bless and care for them and make them into a great nation, and they promised to obey Him. But the good intentions of the people quickly wore off, so God issued the "Ten Commandments" to lead them to a life of practical holiness. He demanded that the people worship no other gods than Him, refrain from making idols or taking his name in vain, and observe the Sabbath as a holy day. He also required them to honor their parents and avoid murder, adultery, stealing, lying, and envy. (Exodus 20)
- The Sermon on the Mount: In the Sermon on the Mount, Jesus demands righteousness in our hearts as well as in our deeds. For example, we are taught not only to avoid murder, but also to avoid anger; not to commit adultery, but also not to look lustfully on another; and other great teachings that help us address our inner beings as well as our behavior. (Matthew 5)
- The Golden Rule: Jesus' teachings often direct us to a good and positive life that honors others and avoids the hurt many of us so often feel or impose on others. These teachings are perhaps best reflected in what we commonly refer to as the "Golden Rule"— "Do for others what you want them to do for you." (Matthew 7:12)

These three great codes are brought together by the great commandment of Matthew 22: 37-39, "Love the Lord your God with all your heart, soul, and mind. This is the first and greatest commandment. The second most important is similar: Love your neighbor as much as you love yourself."

"I realized when I maintain a strong relationship with God I live well. When I apply Biblical truths to my life I am well as a person."

Following these biblical codes will help you help yourself—and your loved one.

Hope

Hope is our quiet, never ending dream for the future. When our present situation is not enough to satisfy us completely, no matter how good or bad, we hunger for more. Our unsatisfied search for more is the basis of biblical hope. Hope is not just a wish or want. Our faith helps us see God working in our past, see our life as it is, and know that He will work in our lives in the future.

How do we use our troubles of the past to hope for a better life, especially if a loved one is locked in prison? Second Corinthians tells the story of Paul, who faced a similar situation. Paul wrote to the church at Corinth about his hard time when he went through Asia: crushed, overwhelmed, and fearful that he would never live through it. He wrote, "We felt we were doomed to die and saw how powerless we were to help ourselves; but that was good, for then we put everything into the hands of God, who alone could save us, for he can even raise the dead. And he did help us, and saved us from a terrible death; yes, and we expect Him to do it again and again." (2 Corinthians 1: 9-10)

"Life in here is very lonely and most people just can't see anything good happening in the future because

the path they have chosen has brought nothing but pain and heart ache on them in the past."

We all have problems, and no one is immune from suffering, from hurting others, from being hurt by others, from broken relationships. However, through faith in God we can make the best of our bad situation and hope for a better future.

"Our hope is in the faith that our salvation through God's promise and His Word will transform our lives so that we can return to our families and society as healthier human beings."

Three influences work to give us hope. First, struggles cause us to pray, and prayer gives us hope. In asking for help we acknowledge our weaknesses, and accept that we need help from God. We acknowledge that His power is without limit. Furthermore, prayer helps us picture success and construct a vision of what our hope really is. When we do this, we believe more strongly and work harder and more intelligently, often in many very small ways, to do our part in making our hopes a reality.

The second influence for hope is that faith in God fosters an early success. Most of us have sinned against God. And all we have to do to heal our relationship with God is to ask. When we do so and feel His presence, we have a success that helps us understand there is reason for hope. Thus, while a hearing, loving, forgiving God is easier to deal with than a hurt, abused human being, mending a relationship with God suggests that mending other broken aspects of our life is possible.

The third influence for hope is that God is constant, and if we believe in Him we know that He will be with us through all our ups and downs. Dealing with incarceration is not easy, and there will be good times and bad. But God is always present and never changes. We can depend on Him and rely on Him for strength when times are tough, and this gives us hope.

Love

A great moral standard and faith-based hope for the future are hollow without love. Two kinds of love are important.

One, need-love, is the love that sends a lonely or frightened child to its mother's arms—and it's the love your incarcerated family member needs from you—and that you also need from him. Need-love is the basis of a person's spiritual life and love for God. It recognizes that we are incomplete, that our whole being is one of great need. It leads offenders to yearn for affection from families, loved ones, and others. Regardless of how unlovable their behavior has been, they can seek love with the certainty that God will love them and with the hope that others will do so as well. Such love can motivate them to make a real effort to improve their lives, because they want to please someone who loves them: parents, siblings, friends, and God.

"And I know you love me too and thank you so much."

Gift-love is God Himself working through a person—in this case, mainly through you. It is goodness exhibited in your relationship with your incarcerated loved one; a love that you have for him even though he has violated your trust, done bad things, and caused you big problems. But he is also God's child, has his own special story and humanity, and his own corner of good. Showing gift-love means you look beyond his faults and show him love that has no agenda and expects nothing in return. Loving your troubled family member is loving God, or as Jesus said in Matthew 25:40, "When you did it to these my brothers you were doing it to me!"

"Tell everyone I miss them and love them."

Showing gift-love to an incarcerated family member will probably be risky. He probably has a very poor track record, which is a recipe for betrayal and distress. Loving someone without a track record is like lending money to a stranger. It's not a safe investment. Unlike lending money, however, the more love we give, the more we have. Loving another who may betray us is like God's love for us. He knows we will let Him down, but He loves us anyway.

A Process for Change

Biblical teachings will guide your loved one as he attempts to deal with his past and change his future, and they will also guide you as you try to help him. The Bible provides a road map for a journey that changes lives and relationships. This road map is the basis of the remainder of this book. The starting point is your looking closely at what you know about your loved one. Doing so will help you see where he is and where he needs to be. Then, you both can follow a biblical process for change. The process—responsibility, accountability, confession, repentance, forgiveness, reconciliation, and restitution—will be more fully developed in future chapters.

"What could I say now? What can I do now to change all this? That's the key—change! I am now doing everything in my power to change. I didn't even like myself and decided, how could anybody else like me and I didn't even like myself?"

NURTURING YOUR LOVED ONE'S FAITH

What if you have a firm belief and a strong faith, but your loved one isn't so sure, or just doesn't buy into all this? What now? How do you deliver the good news that there is a great moral code to guide him, God loves him, and there is hope?

"I associated God with society and cops, so I hated God to. When I was 16 I began proclaiming to worship satan. The satanic mentality took its toll on my perception. If I could've found a satanic church to worship in I would've dove in full force."

Overt evangelizing is fraught with dangers and concerns. There is the risk that your loved one will "convert" temporarily to make you feel better or as part of a hustling game to get more from you, and become a religious criminal rather than a changed person. You cannot force true faith on a loved one. There is a risk that too much evangelizing will be seen as attempted coercion and will backfire.

St. Francis of Assisi suggested we "Preach the Gospel at all times and when necessary use words." This suggests a ministry of presence, where you teach the love of Christ by helping your loved one and demonstrating God's love in your own life. You become a witness of Christ through the natural outcome of living for Him. Your loved one will see a sermon rather than hear one when you model your own faith. Pray, for yourself, for him, and for your family. Pray together with him if he is willing. Read the Bible and live by its moral code, and read it with him if he is willing. Write about your faith in your letters and offer to attend religious services together after his release, always being sensitive to where each of you is during your faith journey and to the potential dangers of too much evangelizing.

Demonstrate Jesus's charge in Matthew 22:34-40 to love your neighbor as yourself: "'Love the Lord your God with all your heart and with all your soul and with all your mind.' This is the first and greatest commandment. And the second is like it: 'Love your neighbor as yourself.'"

Teach a message of love—love that is unconditional, foundational, and unshakeable—given completely and without reservation to God and to your incarcerated loved one. You can be an example of love in many ways: By just being present and treating him with respect and dignity, letting him know you care and will not give up on him, no matter what he has done. By telling him you love him and miss him, consistently. By celebrating and reinforcing his achievements and finding ways to tell him you are proud of him.

"I will follow the letter of the law which for me means staying close to God and trusting Him for all my Spiritual and Physical needs and most importantly, Peace of Mine. Accomplishing this is my goal and is what will allow me to keep my promise to you of never getting in trouble again."

Jesus treated people right, even when they mistreated him or were condemned by society. You can do the same. Your presence alone demonstrates the love and forgiveness that shows how Christianity should really work. And you can work with him through the journey suggested in the following pages.

THINGS TO THINK ABOUT

1. HOW STRONG IS MY FAITH?

2. WHAT MORAL CODE DO I LIVE BY?

3. HOW STRONG DO I BELIEVE MY LOVED ONE'S FAITH IS?

4. HOW CAN I BEST TEACH _____ ABOUT FAITH BY THE WAY I LIVE AND BEHAVE?

5. HOW CAN I BEST FOSTER BIBLICAL HOPE IN MY LOVED ONE?

6. HOW CAN I BEST SHOW HIM OR HER LOVE?

5

STORIES

"I finally told my story. I got a lot out of it. My freedom."

Think again about the crash of the Concorde jet discussed in Chapter 3, and the conclusion that debris on the runway started a chain of events that led to the crash. Now think about what the investigators had to consider before deciding how to prevent such crashes from happening again: the load of the plane, flames shooting from its left wing, a fuel leak, the structure of the tire, and many other factors as well as the debris on the runway. They had to look below the surface, consider many factors, and make many judgments.

Similarly, for your loved one to really change and avoid doing the same things again, he needs to think deeply about his life story and the underlying causes of his behavior, see both the good and the bad, and build a foundation for positive change. To help your loved one change, you also need to see him as he is—as completely, honestly, and objectively as possible. Acknowledge his problems and discern as much as you can about their basic cause(s) before trying to help him.

Your task may be more difficult than an accident investigator's. You probably love him and have a history with him, so you are biased (good or bad) and are personally affected by his life. Your loved one may not want your help and may even resent your attention. He may hide information from you or mislead you. On the other hand, he might be begging for your help. If so, you can count yourself lucky because you both may now be able to begin a new path and grow together. Accurately understanding the situation may be difficult. This chapter should help you with this task. The first part, "Hearing Your Loved One's Story," suggests how to look at the situation. The second part, "Helping Change Your Loved One's Story," suggests what to look at.

HEARING YOUR LOVED ONE'S STORY

Your loved one cannot just fix the obvious broken parts of her life. She needs to address all her behavior, consider the root causes, and reinforce the good while changing the bad. Helping your loved one requires you to be concerned about the same issues as you try to discern her needs. The following tips will guide your efforts.

Maintain a Servant Attitude

Your objective is to serve your loved one. Jesus said, "For even the Son of Man did not come to be served but to serve," (Mark 10:45) and the apostle Paul added, "Each of you should be concerned not only about your own interests, but the interests of others as well." (Philippians 1:4)

The following should help you maintain a servant attitude:

- Accept him as he is. He made mistakes and bad choices, probably hurting you badly along the way. He may have hurt others badly as well. He may be facing judgment from the loved ones he has impacted with his mistakes as well as the community he will return to when released. Get beyond his bad behavior and accept him as a worthy individual, with his own feelings, beliefs, values, aspirations, and life. Create an environment where your loved one feels safe to share and talk about his concerns.

  "Thank you for accepting me as I am."

- Be patient. It takes time for people to change and grow. Give him time to understand himself and find his solutions to his problems. There will be fits and starts, mistakes, start-overs, and such. Work in his time.

- Be honest. Tell your loved one the truth. Be truthful with yourself, and willing to reveal your own concerns and limitations. Be willing to say that you can't—or are not willing to—help in a certain situation. If possible, explain to him why you cannot help, but do not feel you have to

give him an excuse. Honesty leads to trust, and trust makes it more likely the offender will reveal himself and his own problems.
- Seek to meet his needs rather than yours. This doesn't mean disregarding your own well-being, as discussed in Chapter 2. But it does mean that in matters affecting him, you need to willingly give of yourself and strive to meet his needs rather than what you want for yourself or him.
- Be humble. Acknowledge that you don't have all the answers and have much to learn. Be open to new ideas and experiences.

Avoid Controlling Behavior

The causes of crime discussed in Chapter 3 all involve your loved one's behavior—not yours. You can control your behavior, but not hers; not now or after she is released. You can't control her drinking, or her wants, or her anger, or any other aspect of her behavior. You can exert a positive influence, but you have to be careful not to step over the line and try to control her. You may appear to be trying to control a loved one when you believe you are only offering suggestions or advice. If your preferences determine his decisions, he is likely to feel controlled.

People often try to control others because, at some level, they believe they know more or are more capable than the other person. This can easily be the case when family members who are not in prison (and generally have made better choices) are trying to help loved ones who are in prison. Trying to control your loved one can easily lead you to project an air of superiority, objectify him, and appear to try to own him.

You have no right to control your loved one, and you probably couldn't if you did have a right. You can't make him what you want him to be or decide what is best for him. His problems and challenges are ultimately his own, and he needs to accept responsibility and acknowledge that change must come from within. Your goal is to help your loved one discover and use his own abilities to make his own decisions and manage his own life.

Listen

Listening is probably the most important skill you can apply to helping your loved one. It is a way of communicating in which each person involved both receives and sends messages. First, of course, is that effective listening—really hearing what he communicates and taking it to heart—allows you to receive information from your loved one about whether he wants your help, and if so how you can go about it; how he feels, what he likes or dislikes, all the things you need to know in order to focus on him rather than yourself. You begin to see the world as he sees it and "walk in his shoes."

Effective listening often does more to send messages than to receive them. When you listen carefully to your loved one you confirm his self-worth by showing that you value him and his ideas. Failing to listen and respond also tells him something about himself, and is likely to be seen as discounting him. If you ignore him, interrupt him, look stern while he is talking, or make snap judgments about what he is saying, you convey the message that he isn't worth listening to. Such discounting is likely to cause an already low self-esteem to plummet even lower.

Chapter 8 provides information as to how to listen effectively.

Judge Without Condemning

To help an incarcerated loved one, look closely at his entire life, identify to the best of your ability the causes of his criminal activity, and consider how he has reacted to his conviction and incarceration. Honestly get to know him. Learning more about your loved one may not paint a pretty picture. Occasionally innocent people are locked up, but usually people are locked up because they committed crimes. And often they also committed crimes for which they are not incarcerated.

Seeing his life as it is will require honesty, and honesty will no doubt involve judging. Sometimes people object to judging others. After all, Romans 14:13 says, "Therefore let us stop passing judgment on one another." But the Bible and civil society have established standards we all are to live by, and most inmates have obviously failed in doing so. How can one respect those standards and avoid judging? How does one help an inmate get his life together without understanding what he has done and making some judgments about it? The answer is that judgment is necessary to help an offender. You need to help your incarcerated loved one understand where his life went off track, and that making better choices requires judgments about right and wrong, good and bad, and consequences.

The word "judge" is used in two different ways in the New Testament. Sometimes "judge" means sitting in judgment, or even condemning, people. But more often it means to judge between things, to differentiate, or discern—between right and wrong, good and evil, righteous and unrighteous. Christianity does not forbid judgment as an act of discernment. In fact, much Christian teaching suggests that we are supposed to exercise righteous judgment, with careful discernment. The Bible condemns hypocritical, self-righteous judgment of others, not discernment between right and wrong.

It's okay, even advisable, to honestly conclude that your loved one has acted badly and to refuse to justify his inappropriate actions. That is the essence of discernment. But discernment should not cause you to value him less or condemn him. When you condemn a loved one, you declare that he has no value to you or to God. You see him not as a person, but as a thing—less human and therefore less valuable. And once you see your loved one this way, it's easy to convince yourself that you don't have to respect him, serve him, or love him.

Look Also at Yourself

Each offender is part of a family system. His behavior not only affects, but also is affected by, other members of the family. Family members, and their actions, are part of the picture of his life, particularly during that time before he became involved in crime. Family relationships, duties, responsibilities and privileges, attitudes and actions of parents, family crises and other such factors may have contributed to the behavior that led to your loved one's offenses. And such family influences will continue to affect him in the future. Therefore, as you try to help him turn his life around consider whether you should change your own life as well in order to model the behavior you want from him.

"I began making a conscious evaluation of my life good and bad. I was very angry at my father at that time and I was looking at the men he'd been in my life, good & bad. While my father did his best to raise me, and he taught me some very good things, he had problems. Because of his problems I wasn't taught or shown much in the way of self-control, or self-disciplin. My <u>dad's drug addictions</u> could seem insatiable at times when he was young. I had acquired the same type of addiction for weed."

HELPING CHANGE YOUR LOVED ONE'S STORY

Helping your loved one change his life requires you to start from where he is. Understanding where he is requires an in-depth look at several aspects of his life story.

The Positives

You probably don't feel very good about your loved one who is locked up: you may be disappointed, angry, embarrassed, cynical. Perhaps you don't trust him. But never forget that your loved one is a human <u>being who God loves,</u> and there is much good and positive about him. See the good. Your attempts to help him are more likely to be successful if you recognize and build on the good than if you just focus on the problems. This does not mean pretending that all is rosy and there are no problems. Rather, it means acknowledging his bad behavior, but focusing on the good and not condemning him as a person. Think of your good times in the past, of the good things he has done, the fun you have had. Of his intelligence or hard work. Of his spirituality. Of his friendliness. Of the good choices he has made. Of the fact that God loves him. Appreciate your shared humanity, make fair judgments without condemning him. See the glass as half full rather than half empty.

Seeing the good is a self-fulfilling prophesy. If you see only the down side, you will set low expectations. Your loved one will perceive the low expectations, and he will meet them. If you recognize the good and set high expectations, he will usually respond accordingly.

Behavior Before Crime

Hopefully you have concluded that your loved one's life is a glass more than half full, and there is much positive to build on. But he is in prison. Some things have not been so good. These not so good things also are part of your loved one's story, which most likely started well before he committed his first crime.

"I know the journey begins with the choice to commit a crime that's way before a person hits TDC. Sometimes its years before they're arrested."

Most people who are locked up had a pattern of legal but highly inappropriate behavior before committing crimes. Think of the young person who missed too much school, continually ran away from home, or had a pattern of lying or manipulating. Or the person who drank too much, hung out with the wrong people, or couldn't keep a job. Such activities didn't warrant prison time. But they are just as—perhaps more—important considerations in your loved one improving his life than the actual crime.

The past is done and can't be changed. Harping on mistakes of the past will probably only create more problems. But the behavior that led to crime is an essential part of the fabric of who your loved one is. It is part of the life story that he needs to transform. It contains the seeds of the crimes that resulted in incarceration. To avoid repeating past mistakes, your loved one needs to acknowledge and deal with them, as will be discussed in future chapters.

Criminal Activity

Dr. Clara Harris, a Houston area dentist and mother of twin boys, was convicted of first-degree murder and sentenced to 20 years in prison. A jury found she acted with "sudden passion" when she killed her husband by running over him with her Mercedes-Benz. At the trial, the victim's brother testified that Harris was "one of the most law-abiding persons I know."

Apparently this was Harris' first criminal act. More commonly people are not locked up for their first or only crime, and sometimes not even for the crime they actually committed. Sometimes they weren't caught in their earlier crimes. Sometimes they got caught, were convicted—perhaps "only" of a misdemeanor—and were given probation and a second chance. Sometimes they admitted to a lesser offense in a plea bargain. Regardless of the situation, people in prison usually have committed more crimes than their crime of record. How may armed robberies are preceded by simple burglary? How many of all crimes are preceded by various drug offenses?

"When I turned 15 years old, I had ran away from home so many times, my parents wouldn't even give me any money anymore because they knew that I would just go buy drugs with it. So one day after I was about 15 ½ years old, I went to my Dad with a couple friends and ask him for $20.00 and he ran me off and told me not to bring them drug heads back around his house. So with my sick

way of thinking, because my dad wouldn't give me any money, I thought that I could hurt him by going and robbing a store. So I robbed an old country store."

Other criminal activity is usually part of the chain of offenses leading to your loved one's crime of record, and is also part of the fabric of who he is. Similarly, all of his past behavior comprises the life story he needs to transform if he is to avoid returning to prison after his release.

Behavior in Prison

Prison affects people, sometimes for the better but often for the worse. Personal change is inevitable as an inmate either fights the system or learns to adapt to it. And the longer he's locked up, the greater the change.

Seeing the change in a loved one who is locked behind bars can be a challenge. But remember, to help your loved one you have to deal with the person he is now and not with the person you remember.

"When a man goes to prison everything changes for him. He feels powerless where he use to be in control and it's almost like everything he was trained to be—his duties as a man, are ripped away from him. This type of man feels dead because he has no control in areas where he use to."

There is an old story about a farmer selling his mule. The potential buyer asked if the mule was a good worker that obeyed every command. The owner replied yes to both questions. To prove it he got the mule into his harness and yelled "giddy-up." The mule just stood there. The farmer tried a couple of more times with no success. The buyer looked at the owner and said, "I thought you told me this mule obeys." "He does," says the owner, who then picked up a 2x4, walked to the front of the mule, and hit him as hard as he could, right between the eyes. Then he softly said "giddy-up" and the mule obeyed, much to the surprise of the buyer. The owner explained, "This mule always obeys, but sometimes you gotta get his attention first."

Sometimes prison is like a 2x4 between the eyes for a person who has committed crimes. Prison works like it is supposed to, gets the offender's attention, and provides incentive and opportunity for positive change. Perhaps he was first locked up when he was a young person in the "high crime" age bracket, and has now matured. Hopefully he has turned his back on drugs, violence, and other more youthful indiscretions. He may have developed his spirituality, or even enhanced his life skills or job qualifications by taking advantage of opportunities made available by the system.

"Sometimes I don't think I've gotten very far in changing since I've been locked up and I'm like, 'Is any of this worth it?' Other times I know I've made some progress."

Often, however, the prison experience is not so positive, and he may have changed in the opposite direction. He may have fallen into a widely acknowledged pattern of criminal thinking. He begins to think like a victim, where he continually blames others for his own situation, claims he is the one who was really wronged, and believes no one in the world has experienced what he has experienced. He refuses to take responsibility for what he has done and assumes that others are out to get him. He spends a lot of time trying to figure out other peoples' angles. Those involved in criminal thinking typically make choices based on what they wish were true rather than what is true, and try to act fearless but in fact live in fear. Unfortunately, actual behavior can also deteriorate. Inmates may learn from their surroundings to be better, more accomplished criminals. They may become involved in activities such as gaming the system, hustling, petty thievery, violence, or prison gangs. They may sink deeper into the morass than when they were initially locked up.

"I wanted out so bad. I used every I'm gonna I could possibly think: I'm gonna stay off drugs, I'm gonna work and get a lawyer, I'm gonna, I'm gonna. I was so manipulative I fooled myself."

Regardless of how your loved one has changed since going to prison, his current thinking patterns and behavior are critical in any effort for a restored life.

To change his life, your loved one has to deal with the person he is at the present time—not the person who committed the crime that took him to prison. If you are to help him, you have to acknowledge the same person. But regardless of where he is now, pursuing a restored life requires him to deal with the consequences of his past. This takes us to a consideration of "Responsibility," the topic of Chapter 6.

THINGS TO THINK ABOUT

1. AT LEAST FIVE THINGS THAT ARE GOOD ABOUT _____ AND THAT HE CAN BUILD ON TO TURN HIS LIFE AROUND ARE:

2. THREE CHARACTERISTICS OR EVENTS I AM AWARE OF IN _____'S EARLY LIFE THAT COULD HAVE BEEN THE ROOT CAUSE OF HIS CRIME:

3. HIS CRIME OF RECORD IS: _____

4. I KNOW OR SUSPECT THAT _____ HAS COMMITTED THE FOLLOWING ADDITIONAL CRIMES:

5. I NEED TO CONSIDER THE FOLLOWING CHANGES IN MY OWN LIFE IN ORDER TO REALLY HELP _____:

6

RESPONSIBILITY

"I can now understand there is a chain reaction that starts with me."

Janus, the god of beginnings and transitions in ancient Roman religion and myth, is represented by a double-faced head, each looking in opposite directions. It was said that he could see into the past with one face and into the future with the other. Hence, Janus was worshipped at the beginnings of the harvest and planting times, as well as at marriages, deaths, and other important transitions in people's lives. Your incarcerated loved one is facing an important transition and hopefully an equally important beginning in his life. I don't suggest worshipping this Roman god as part of the transition. But I do suggest you look both backward and forward as you think about "responsibility" and how it plays both backward and forward in his life.

Looking back, your loved one's actions have no doubt had major, often negative, effects on a number of others. He is responsible for these consequences of his past actions. Looking forward, he needs to take care of many things in the future. He is responsible for them. To truly transform his life, he needs to deal with responsibility from both perspectives.

LOOKING BACK AND DEALING WITH CONSEQUENCES

Thinking about the story of David and Bathsheba from 2 Samuel 11-13 helps us look back on the concept of responsibility. David, king of Israel, committed adultery with Bathsheba. He tried to cover up the adultery by having her husband, Uriah, assigned to the front lines of battle, where he was killed as expected. David then married Bathsheba, and they had a son, but the Lord killed him as punishment for David's sin. Amnon, David's first-born son (by another wife) conspired with his cousin, Jonadab, to get Tamar (his half-sister, David's daughter by still another wife) into bed. When his plan didn't work, he raped her and then threw her out. This greatly angered Absalom, Tamar's brother and another of David's sons, so he had his men kill Amnon. Absalom then incited a rebellion against David, and on and on. What a mess!

Think about David, the consequences of his behavior, and all the people his actions affected. He committed adultery with Bathsheba and in effect murdered Uriah. But the matter didn't stop with these direct actions. He was responsible for the Lord taking his son's life. Perhaps he also was at least partially responsible for Tamar's rape because of the example he set for Amnon. Didn't he have some responsibility for the entire dismal chain of events in his family? Clearly, his bad behavior rippled out well beyond his adultery and murder, and affected his entire family. And similarly, your loved one's behavior no doubt has had negative consequences that are broad and deep.

What Responsibility Is

Responsibility is about cause and effect. Cause is the reason something happens. Effect—also called consequence—is the result. We often think of cause and effect (or consequence) as a simple process, where "x" causes "y", and that's about it. Offenders are prone to such thinking and therefore frequently fail to recognize the magnitude of what they have done or the number of lives (victims) they have affected. They often maintain that their behavior had no, or very limited, effects or consequences. For example, they frequently see drug crimes as victimless, property crimes like theft and burglary as inconsequential because the victims are "rich" or deserved it, and crimes such as assault and murder as affecting only the individuals who were assaulted or murdered.

But life is not so simple—as we saw in the case of King David and his family—and the consequences of crime spread like the waves that ripple out when you throw a rock into a still pond.

Direct victims are usually hit hardest by offenders' actions. Their families, loved ones, and friends (including you) also suffer the consequences: loss or impairment of a strong emotional connection, financial suffering, and all the other effects of having a loved one hurt or killed or incarcerated. Seemingly minor property crimes affect all of society and all of us as individuals when prices, insurance costs, and policing costs go up. Drug use—perhaps that encouraged by just one user or dealer—imposes incredible personal and social consequences on unseen children, families, and all of us. As a family member of a loved one who is incarcerated, you understand the ripple effect of his actions on you and your family: the embarrassment, the emotional strain, the financial problems, and on and on.

"Unfortunately, I know that many people were hurt by the events which led to my eventual incarceration. I would give anything to be able to rewind the clock and handle my situation a different way. Of course, that is impossible. I am stuck like the rest of the world with living with the consequences of my decisions."

In this confusing and complex world, should the offender always be responsible for such consequences? Sometimes family members and other loved ones have done things that led to an offender's actions. And what about failures of society, like poverty, racism, poor schools, and mis-directed government policy? Don't all these problems mean the offender should not be blamed? Is he really responsible when society and others helped make him who he is?

The answer boils down to a matter of choice. When we freely choose to do something or not to do something, we are responsible for the consequences of that choice. Offenders nearly always have free choice about their decisions. A few may commit crimes because they are forced to do so. Sometimes psychologists and neuroscientists argue that people are driven to commit crimes by forces beyond their conscious control. However, except in the rare case of physical force or certain mental illnesses, those who commit crimes do so from their own free will. Many life experiences make living straight more difficult or life unfair. However, without minimizing the difficulty of life or even its essential unfairness, one can say that nearly all offenders had a choice about what they did. And your loved one probably had a choice about what he did. So he is responsible for the consequences.

Accepting Responsibility

Accepting responsibility for one's actions is the first step in a longer process that involves a number of principles discussed in later chapters of this book: being accountable, confessing, and repenting provide overwhelming evidence that one has accepted responsibility. For now, it's helpful to view accepting responsibility as simply looking back and acknowledging guilt and the consequences of one's past actions, and demonstrating behavior consistent with doing something about those consequences.

Isn't taking responsibility for the past just a form of "Monday morning quarterbacking" that allows criticism, blame, guilt, or passing the buck? Doesn't considering his responsibility just cause hope for a better past that really isn't there? Shouldn't he just forget the past and move on to a better future?

Certainly, the past is over, and your loved one cannot change what he has done. But the importance of his accepting responsibility for the consequences of what he has done cannot be underestimated. Think of his mind as a stagnated, hard-packed garden, and new and different ideas as seeds. His act of accepting responsibility works like turning nutrient rich compost into the soil. Like compost softens and opens the soil to receive the seed, taking responsibility opens his mind and prepares it for new ideas. It helps change his criminal mind to an open one where transformative ideas and lessons can take root and grow.

Taking responsibility helps him realize that every effect (on his victims) had a cause (his actions), and that acknowledging the effects of his past behavior is not a form of weakness. Rather, it is a form of strength and self-acceptance that avoids denial, rationalization, and blame. When he accepts responsibility he recognizes that his problems are his own, he has power over his life and behavior, and he can control them. And nothing is more empowering than realizing he is in control of his life.

"I didn't fully accept and carry-out these responsibilities based on choices and behaviors of my past. That has caused so much pain and embarrassment to you'all and others in society."

Helping Your Loved One Accept Responsibility

How do you help a loved one accept and acknowledge responsibility for the consequences of his past? You walk a tightrope: acknowledge his guilt without fostering an immobilizing shame, encourage sincere remorse without wasting time trying to alter the past, show an interest in your loved one's restoration without being seen as manipulative or overbearing.

The place to start is to make a judgment about the extent to which you may have contributed to your loved one's offenses or are currently contributing to his failure to take responsibility for their consequences. A simple example can help you think about your possible contribution—and responsibility. Anyone who caused an accident while intoxicated is responsible for the damages to innocent victims. In addition, however, those who provided the alcohol—such as bar owners or parents—are often considered at fault and ultimately held responsible as well because they served the liquor when they knew or should have known that problems were likely to result. Similarly, your incarcerated loved one is responsible for the consequences of his crime. But family members may also bear some responsibility.

Look honestly and closely at yourself. Have you provided a bad role model or done other things that taught him the wrong life lessons and made living in accordance with the law more difficult than it should have been? Are you still doing these things? If so, address your own actions. Live like you want him to live when he is released.

You can also help your loved one accept responsibility by refusing to play his games. Offenders—really any of us—who fail to take responsibility for their actions typically engage in one or more of the following:

- Denial: We hide from ourselves, repress our actions in our unconscious, pretend things didn't happen, or convince ourselves that consequences did not result. We don't see ourselves as we really are.
- Rationalization: We allow our minds to construct false explanations or minimize the consequences of our actions. We tell our self that we really didn't have a choice or that our behavior really wasn't so bad.
- Blame: We try to shift responsibility to someone else. We see our bad behavior as someone else's fault.

If your loved one denies that he caused the consequences of his actions, tries to rationalize the consequences away, or unfairly blames another for what he did, he is not facing up to his responsibility. If you go along with any of these types of intellectual dishonesty, you are complicit in his failure to take responsibility.

"I want to take responsibility for a burglary I have not been charged with. It hit me Thursday night and I cried very hard. It's the burglary that I got the necklace from that I associate with [a particular] story. It's only right that I take responsibility for this crime I committed since her assailent never came forward."

Refusing to play his games and encouraging him to take responsibility can backfire. Your action can make his denial firmer or give him someone else to blame. Thus, go slow and consider whether he can handle your involvement. What you do should depend on the circumstances: whether your loved one is a juvenile or a seasoned veteran, how your relationship with him works, the type of crime he committed, how long he will be locked up, and other similar considerations. As you formulate your approach, consider the following:

- Be honest with yourself about your loved one's actions, their consequences, and the harm he has done. You cannot help your loved one accept responsibility if you don't believe he should be responsible. Think again about the discussion in Chapter 5 concerning judging without condemning. Discern what hurt he caused—honestly, without condemning him for it.
- Remember that she probably wants validation, not correction, from you. And she doesn't want to feel judged, misunderstood, or forced into believing something she is not ready to believe. Be careful to validate her as a person, while at the same time refusing to confirm or enable her denial, rationalizing, or blaming. Convince her she is a good person, even if she has done bad things.
- Check your own feelings. It's quite likely that you are one of the victims your loved one is not acknowledging he hurt. Manage to put that behind you, and address your loved one's issues rather than your own agenda.
- Convince him that, notwithstanding the bars, he is a free person, in control of important parts of his life. Freedom is not the right to do as he pleases. It is the power and capacity to decide what he ought to do under the circumstances and to do it. Freedom is the ability to choose what attitude will govern his life and to take responsibility

for the right choices. And it is the ability to adopt new attitudes rather than hold on to old ones.

- Convey a sense of his responsibility in the subtle messages you give him in your letters, talks, questions, and comments. Convey the message that it was him, not external forces, who was in charge when he committed his crime, and that his crime did in fact affect a number of others.
- Do your best to discern whether your relationship allows you to be more direct. If so, directly question his lack of responsibility and give him advice. If you conclude that such intervention will be okay, proceed slowly and with great care.
- Praise him when he acknowledges his responsibility. Use such opportunities to give some encouragement or discuss the situation with him.

Hopefully your loved one will pass the test of being responsible by being accountable to others, confessing what he has done, and repenting or changing his life. These will be discussed in more detail in later chapters. Let's now look to his responsibility for future behavior.

LOOKING FORWARD AND BEING RESPONSIBLE

We noted earlier that accepting responsibility for the consequences of past actions helps your loved one look to the future and accept responsibility for shaping it. Your loved one should not just re-arrange the deck chairs on the Titanic—or just keep on doing the same things, perhaps a little better. Instead, he should shift his focus from denying, rationalizing, and blaming toward taking personal control of his life and doing those things that successful citizens do: such as getting beyond the mindset that led to his criminal activity, depending on himself rather than others, setting a realistic direction and plan for his life, beginning to make right choices, and acknowledging his failures and celebrating his successes. And he should do more concrete, measurable things such as improving his education, addressing addiction, improving relationships with loved ones, and making plans for life after release.

Helping your loved one do such things can make matters worse if you create or exacerbate a problematic dependency, or if you are seen as meddling or trying to control him. But you can try to hold him accountable for taking care of his own responsibilities, which is the subject of the next chapter.

THINGS TO THINK ABOUT

1. SEVERAL IMPORTANT CONSEQUENCES OF _____'S CRIME AND INCARCERATION ARE:

2. THE FOLLOWING BEHAVIOR SUGGESTS THAT _____ HAS/HAS NOT ACCEPTED RESPONSIBILITY FOR HIS ACTIONS:

3. I WILL DO THE FOLLOWING TO VALIDATE _____:

4. I CAN DO THE FOLLOWING—WITHOUT UNDUE RISK OF CREATING ADDITIONAL PROBLEMS—TO ENCOURAGE HIM TO ACCEPT RESPONSIBILITY FOR THE CONSEQUENCES OF HIS PAST ACTIONS:

5. I HOPE _____ WILL BE RESPONSIBLE FOR THE FOLLOWING IN THE FUTURE:

7

ACCOUNTABILITY

"It gave me the chance to open up and let my heart speak to the victims on a personal basis."

Let's continue the story of David, Bathsheba, and David's family, introduced in Chapter 6. David committed adultery with Bathsheba, had her husband murdered, and raised sons who committed rape and murder and rebelled against the family. The story continues in Psalm 51, where David admits his shameful deeds and acknowledges that although Bathsheba, her husband, and his family were his direct victims, he has also sinned against God. He has hurt others but must answer to God because he has rebelled against His laws and ways of living. Because David is accountable to God, he admits his sins to Him, accepts his punishment, asks for forgiveness, and offers penance.

Accountability means being answerable and implies a legal, moral, or other obligation to someone as though he is sitting in judgment and can in some way call you to account. Accountability is closely related to responsibility. Responsibility is largely a matter of one's behavior and its consequences, while accountability is based on rules, expectations, or judgments by yourself and others about answering for that behavior. Responsibility involves what one does or does not do and the effects of such behavior. Accountability involves answering for what one has done or failed to do.

"I have cleaned up my messy life and want to do my best to fix what I screwed up and what I ruined in their lives and in their hearts. I owe them that change in me and I owe them that peace."

Accountability may arise from a formal relationship, such as our obligations under the law or a specific, written contract. For example, we are answerable to the state (police, judges, probation or parole officers, and others) to obey its laws, to a creditor to repay a loan, or to a business partner to fulfill a contract. More often, however, accountability is informal, based on relationships and unstated expectations of those we care about or love and those who care about or love us. We are accountable to God, family, friends, and in many cases even strangers to do what is right. Thus, being accountable involves recognizing the valid need, expectation, or right of another person. Like responsibility, accountability looks both backward and forward. We are being accountable when we answer for past mistakes and recognize our obligation to make things right with those who have a legitimate expectation of us. And we are also being accountable when we acknowledge a current or future responsibility and do what is appropriate to fulfill it.

Accountability requires action that responds to someone, such as addressing a loved one's legitimate needs, or handling a debt properly, or doing what the boss is paying you to do. Being accountable frequently requires actions of the type discussed in more detail in future chapters. For example, confessing to someone, or repenting, or asking for forgiveness, or various forms of restitution are nearly always excellent ways of demonstrating accountability. But here we will boil it down to two important aspects: your need to be accountable to your loved one, and how you can help your incarcerated loved one be accountable to himself and others.

BEING ACCOUNTABLE TO YOUR LOVED ONE

If you want to help your incarcerated loved one be accountable, start by being accountable yourself—for your own actions, responsibilities, and goals. This means following through with your commitments and responsibilities—doing what you know you should do, when you should do it—in your life generally and in your relationship with your loved one.

Being Accountable for the Past

As previously discussed, family relationships, duties, responsibilities, privileges, attitudes, actions, crises and other such factors may have contributed to your loved one's offenses. Look at your own role in these matters. Think about the extent to which you and your past way of life may have contributed to your loved one's offenses, or are currently contributing to his failure to take responsibility for their consequences. If you made mistakes that affected your loved one, don't deny what happened, blame others, make excuses, or try to rationalize the consequences. Step up, take the heat, and do your best to make it right. Some guidelines:

- Tell the truth. Everybody messes up sometimes. Be honest with yourself if you have done things that contributed to your loved ones problems. Lying about it—to yourself or to your loved one—or trying to cover it up always makes it worse.
- If you have made mistakes, change your behavior now. If you were an absentee parent, be present now. If you were not reliable, begin honoring your commitments. If you used too much alcohol, stop. And on and on. Even though your loved one is locked in prison, your actions continue to affect him and his behavior. Changing—acting responsibly in the future—will change the influences on him and give your loved one a role model for success.
- Come to terms with him about your mistakes of the past. Openly discuss things you may have done that contributed to his behavior, and apologize if appropriate. This is, in effect, a form of confession. Chapter 8 will provide some guidance on how to go about it.
- Don't allow your accountability for your actions to let your loved one off the hook for his bad actions. Remember the example in Chapter 6—the person who sold the booze may have some responsibility, but the person most responsible, and accountable, is the one who drank it, drove the car, and

killed someone. You may have done some things you regret, but your loved one did the crime and he needs to be honest with himself and be accountable for his actions.

> *"[It] opened up old wounds from my past that made me aware of family issues from my childhood and how much of a impact it had on my life. ... I'm sure I will learn much more about myself & how I ended up in this situation. Being honest with myself has been a good place to begin."*

Being Accountable For the Present

Accountability often is informal, based on relationships and unstated expectations of those you care about or love and those who care about or love you. Thus, you owe it to your loved one to meet his reasonable expectations, and your loved one should be able to expect a reasonable level of attention and support.

> *"An inmate's most important and personal group of relationships, with loved ones, becomes volatile after incarceration forms barriers between the inmate and his/her loved ones. 99% of the time this is the most stressful factor of being in prison; seperation from loved ones. You could probably call it a form of the broken home syndrom. As an inmate, we spend lots of time in communication with loved ones: writing letters, calling, visiting...Our lives center around such things."*

Balance his needs with yours and the burden on you, and consider where you may need to be accountable, such as:
- Are you living as a role model for him? Does your life encourage or discourage his being accountable?
- Do you write him as often as you can and should?

"Im sure Ive said enough. Hopefully I hear from you soon. Write back! Good mail (Well any mail) is hard to come by these days. Thanks for everything"

- Do you visit him as often as you can and should?
- Do you put a reasonable amount of money on his books, to the extent you are financially able to do so?
- Do you pray with and for him?
- Do you do other things that will make his life better and increase the likelihood of his never returning to prison again after he is released?

"A man in prison with no outside help is drifting aimlessly about, totally at the mercy of a corrupt and evil administration. Because they are indigent or without money on their account to spend at the commissary, they are forced to live on only the necessities we receive,...How do you get the necessities? You have to hustle. How do you do that?...They are all against the rules. So you're always risking disciplinary action which eventually has an impact on your parole decision."

In summary, your relationship with your loved one presumably is based on love! That means you should treat him accordingly.

HELPING YOUR LOVED ONE BE ACCOUNTABLE

"As iron sharpens iron, so one man sharpens another." These words from Proverbs 27:17 suggest our need to "hold" one another accountable. And yet, the notion of holding a loved one accountable seems confusing. How can you "hold" anyone else accountable? Shouldn't he be accountable on his own for things he did or things he should do? He needs to be accountable to many people—often many people you don't even know. Isn't the act of "holding someone accountable" really like threatening him with punishment if he does not do what he knows to be right—or, even worse, what you believe is right? And doesn't the notion of holding another accountable tend to contribute to a sense of "holier than thou," as she who holds another accountable may project an air of being smarter, more righteous, or more powerful, because the other is assumed to owe her an explanation or justification for falling short of the mark?

Your loved one probably does not have a good track record in matters of accountability. To "hold" him accountable, simply support him in fulfilling his responsibilities and effectively living an accountable life. Give him a jump-start and help him learn to be accountable on his own. It's up to him to answer for his past and for what he is doing in the present. You can't do these things for him. If you have to continually remind him he is accountable, it will grow old fast and your relationship will deteriorate.

Start by thinking of who he should be accountable to. Consider a wide range of people or entities, and different ones under different circumstances. Some of the most important are as follows:

- God: Does your loved one answer to God with a faith that will help him in the difficult times? How does he live that faith?
- Himself: He probably has a conscience that knows right and wrong. How does he answer to that conscience?

> *"The separation, then personally living with the shame and guilt every day. When I look around at my environment, I'm constantly reminded of my mistakes. And every night my mistakes throughout life are a barrage assaulting any sense of peace I might have felt over the course of the day."*

- His victim(s): He may be prohibited from contacting his victims, and may not even know who they are. How does he demonstrate his accountability in such situations?

- You: Do you have a relationship that allows him to show that he is accountable to you? Do you make it easy or hard for him to answer to you? Does he answer to you?
- His entire family: Are there "black sheep" who have been negative influences whom he should avoid rather than answer to?
- His friends: Who has helped him and who has led him down the wrong path? Should he answer to the later or separate himself from them?
- Prison officials: Can being accountable to them make his life better? If so, how?
- Parole officers and other law enforcement (after release): How does he insure he will not return to prison?

Hopefully your loved one doesn't deny, make excuses, or rationalize what he has done—but instead acknowledges his past and answers for it. And perhaps he has a good track record of answering to judicial and prison authorities, loved ones, and others on a day-to-day basis. If this is so, he doesn't need much help in being accountable. Reinforce what he is doing. Listen to what he says, acknowledge his bad behavior, confirm his efforts to be accountable, and affirm him as a human being without excusing his criminal behavior or condemning him as a person. Tell him how pleased you are that he is being accountable for his life, and that you love him and will love him regardless.

"I can't begin to convey how much the opportunity to ... hear the results of our own crimes recounted, to see how inhumanly we acted, yet receive forgiveness in place of condemnation and the tools for healing—that is life changing for me. An affirmation of my humanness that I was not even aware I needed ..."

On the other hand, if your loved one denies, makes excuses, or rationalizes his actions or their consequences; or if he continues to disregard his legitimate obligations, your task is more difficult. Try to remind without harping, challenge without accusing, teach without lecturing, confront what he has done without confronting his humanity. Some suggestions:

- Act out of love and respect. He no doubt did bad things that he needs to be accountable for, and that you don't like or respect. But you can still view him as a human being who God loves, and love and respect him in the same way. Show your love and respect in what you do and don't do.
- Be accountable to him. If you have hurt him, influenced his bad behavior, or simply set a bad example for him, own up to your actions. This will model accountability and possibly set in motion a series of reciprocal actions where he responds to your being accountable by being more accountable himself.
- Address his past without harping on it. Your loved one should be accountable for what he has done as well as for what he will do. Helping him be accountable for his past requires you to be interested enough to accept him as he is, and at the same time help him realize that to really change from the past he needs to answer for it. Find non-threatening opportunities to ask him how he is dealing with his past actions or point out good opportunities for him to do so.
- Expect him to do what he says he will do. Insisting he deliver on current commitments is probably the best opportunity you may have to build accountability without appearing to meddle, harp on the past, or be overly critical. Discussing a specific situation may provide a teaching moment for discussing broader accountability concerns.
- Don't buy into his criminal thinking. Chapter 5 noted that inmates often think like a victim, blame others for their own situation, claim they are the one who was really wronged, and refuse to acknowledge or be accountable for what they have done and for what they are doing. Be aware

of his thinking patterns. Confront your loved one and take him out of his comfort zone if he starts to play the role of victim rather than be accountable.

- Encourage a "to-do" list of specific goals. The list might include things such as coming clean with an elderly grandfather or other relative, talking to the prison chaplain about his life, targeting no disciplinary action over a specified time period, or complying with all parole requirements.
- Provide actual, physical help when appropriate. Sometimes a person may want to be accountable but just doesn't have the means: for example, he may not have the money to pay a creditor, or transportation to be at work on time, or report to his parole officer. In such cases, your help may be actual physical help such as a loan or a ride or other assistance that allows him to answer a legitimate obligation.

Confession is the critical starting point for being accountable for one's past. It's the topic of Chapter 8.

THINGS TO THINK ABOUT

1. TO SHOW THAT I AM ACCOUNTABLE TO MY INCARCERATED LOVED ONE, I WILL DO THE FOLLOWING:

2. THE FOLLOWING BEHAVIOR SUGGESTS THAT _____ IS/IS NOT BEING ACCOUNTABLE FOR HIS PAST OR PRESENT ACTIONS:

3. I BELIEVE THE FOLLOWING THREE PERSONS OR ENTITIES ARE THE MOST IMPORTANT FOR _____ TO ANSWER TO:

4. I CAN DO THE FOLLOWING—WITHOUT UNDUE RISK OF CREATING ADDITIONAL PROBLEMS—TO HELP HIM BE ACCOUNTABLE TO THESE PERSONS OR ENTITIES:

5. I WILL AFFIRM AND ENCOURAGE _____ BY DOING THE FOLLOWING:

8

CONFESSION

"I am so sorry."

The story of the Prodigal Son from Luke 15 demonstrates the power of confession and provides a basis for this chapter.

A man had two sons. When the younger told his father, "I want my share of your estate now, instead of waiting until you die!" his father agreed to divide his wealth between his sons.

A few days later this younger son packed all his belongings and took a trip to a distant land, and there wasted all his money on parties and prostitutes. About the time his money was gone a great famine swept over the land, and he began to starve. He persuaded a local farmer to hire him to feed his pigs. The boy became so hungry that even the pods he was feeding the swine looked good to him. And no one gave him anything.

When he finally came to his senses, he said to himself, "At home even the hired men have food enough and to spare, and here I am, dying of hunger! I will go home to my father and say, "Father, I have sinned against both heaven and you, and am no longer worthy of being called your son. Please take me on as a hired man.'"

So he returned home to his father. And while he was still a long distance away, his father saw him coming, and was filled with loving pity and ran and embraced him and kissed him.

His son said to him, "Father, I have sinned against heaven and you, and am not worthy of being called your son."

But his father said to the slaves, "Quick! Bring the finest robe in the house and put it on him. And a jeweled ring for his finger; and shoes! And kill the calf we have in the fattening pen. We must celebrate with a feast, for this son of mine was dead and has returned to life. He was lost and is found." So the party began.

The prodigal son confessed to his father. Confessing means admitting we have been wrong and acknowledging or disclosing our misdeeds, faults, or sins, just as the prodigal son did. We make a good, ol' fashioned apology. Confessing follows accepting responsibility and being accountable for bad behavior of the past. It's a logical next step, the "proof of the pudding."

Many incarcerated offenders confessed their crimes as part of the judicial process, either during an initial investigation or as part of a plea bargain. But this type of confession typically is under pressure and doesn't recognize those who were hurt, or apologize for the bad behavior. It may or may not be honestly felt, and is no indication that the offender has taken responsibility for the consequences of what he did.

True confession is about an offender being honest in dealing with what he has done, apologizing for it, and communicating that he is ready to take the consequences. One who confesses does not deny what he did, rationalize it, or blame others. He clearly affirms that he is guilty, has accepted responsibility, and is accountable for his actions.

Confession is necessary for your loved one to deal with his guilt and develop a sense of wholeness, integrity, and community that can be a foundation for a new and different life. It requires more than admitting guilt because doing so is in his immediate short-term interest. He confesses to himself by being intellectually honest about his faults, shortcomings, and behavior. He confesses to God by acknowledging his sins and beginning to restore relations with Him. He confesses to other people (perhaps you and other loved ones) by being a vulnerable human who is willing to take the risks of being accountable for his shortcomings.

"Dear Rhonda,

I've told you a 100 + I'm sorry. All the $ I wasted on other girls when God had given me the most perfect Christian wife ... how could I have been so BLIND! All the *ts I cheated on you ... when in retrospect ...you're all I needed! Or all the $ I wasted on drugs. "*

When your loved one confesses he may reveal something the hearer doesn't already know. For example, he might reveal additional crimes for the first time. Confession also is a way of communicating that he is accepting responsibility and being accountable for actions that others are already aware of. For example, he might confess a crime for which he was publicly convicted by personally owning up to it and apologizing for its consequences.

Saying "I was wrong, and I am sorry" takes more guts than many people have. You cannot confess for your loved one or force him to confess to you or others. But you can provide an environment that provides him opportunities and encourages him to confess to you. You can do this by being a role model, being present, and listening.

"I was wrong for putting a gun in your face and threatening you. I was wrong for taking your hard earned money. I had no right to cause you to feel any of the emotions you felt that day or any negative emotions that you have felt since then that are linked to my actions. I apologize for any of the negative emotions that have come about because of my actions towards you."

BEING A ROLE MODEL

Chapter 6, "Responsibility," encouraged you to consider whether you and your way of life may have contributed to your loved one's offenses. If you honestly concluded that you may have contributed to his bad behavior, think about taking the lead and confessing to him. Even if your life has been a positive influence, you probably have made mistakes from time to time. All of us do. Consider confessing to him about one (or more) of you mistakes. Confessing your shortcomings will demonstrate that confessing is okay—and may lead to a tit-for-tat response where he confesses in response to your confession. And hearing your confession can help teach him how to confess.

Your confession (and hopefully his as well) will be most beneficial if you follow these suggestions:
- Be honest. Don't confess unless you genuinely believe you have made mistakes and owe an apology. And be honest with your emotions. Confession usually involves guilt, shame, fear, uncertainty, pride, pain, or other similarly difficult feelings. Let your honest emotions show and accept those of the person you are confessing to.
- Be fully accountable. Confess first to yourself and affirm your responsibility for your actions. Don't try to deny what you have done or rationalize away the consequences. Do not shift blame or assign excuses, as this will only begin a negative cycle and make matters worse.
- Be specific. Simply saying a blanket "I'm sorry" is not an effective confession and will do little to build the trust, wholeness, and community that you are seeking. Generalities and often-used comments seem insincere, and they build cynicism rather than trust, push apart rather than bring together, hurt rather than heal. Confessions need to be detailed and specific.
- Demonstrate humility. If you are arrogant or let your pride show, your confession will not work.
- Show respect to the one to whom you are confessing. Respect relates to how you see the other person rather than how you show yourself. It means treating the other person as you want to be treated. It's necessary for an effective confession.

In summary, if you feel a need to confess use the biblical prodigal son as a model for doing so.

BEING PRESENT

Confession requires communication, and your loved one cannot confess to you unless you are present, physically and psychologically, to receive his confession. Being present for an incarcerated loved one isn't easy. How can you be present for someone who is locked away in prison where physical contact is limited or not allowed, and even phone calls are prohibited or severely limited?

You have relatively few opportunities to be physically present with your loved one, and there are many reasons—or perhaps excuses—for not taking advantage of those that do exist. Notwithstanding the difficulties, arrange as many visits and communicate as much as feasible under the circumstances. Write your loved one often—even if he doesn't write back. If phone calls are allowed, use them. Provide him opportunities to confess his crimes (as appropriate considering his situation in the judicial system) and problems if he wants to.

"Interaction with people outside of prison is what most inmates commonly lack and want more than anything else. Interaction is a communication bond, it's a type of relationship that's a keen aspect of development in regards to rehabilitation."

Use every available opportunity to communicate your mental and emotional presence. Acknowledge your loved one's existence and needs. Show that you value and respect him, and are sensitive to his situation. Interact with him as if each of you has nothing to hide, nothing to prove, and nothing to lose.

- Be open to dealing with the past. "Being present" is often related to not worrying about the past and focusing on today. And yet—confession at its core deals with the past: being responsible, accountable, and apologizing for what we have done. An offender who has failed to live up to society's norms has to deal with his troubled past and put it behind him before he can move to an acceptable present.

Recognize this need and make it as easy as possible for your loved one to honestly discuss his past.
- Seek peace first and confession after that. This may seem backwards. You may want your loved one to confess or change his behavior before you are much interested in peace. And finding peace may not be easy in the difficult, stressful, anxious situations that naturally accompany incarceration. But the fact is that peace—not just an absence of conflict, but true peace that includes real harmony and safety in your relationship—leads to positive change and confession rather than vice-versa.
- Be emotionally present. Acknowledge your own emotions and express what you're feeling when you are feeling it without being uncomfortable. Be okay with feeling vulnerable, angry, sad, disappointed, hurt, or other such emotions. Be willing to discuss them without blaming, condemning, or excusing your loved one or yourself. Share positive emotions, such as happiness, love, and caring. Weep. Be uncomfortable. Always show up. Stay. Recognize that your loved one has similar emotions. Accept them as legitimate without engaging in cycles of judging, blaming, and accusing.

Perhaps the most important factor in being present is listening. This is so important that a special section will be devoted to it.

LISTENING

Philosophers and scientists have for years asked the question, "If a tree falls in the woods and there's no one around to hear it, does it make a sound?" Many have concluded no; someone must be present to hear the crash. Similarly, someone needs to hear a "confession" for it to be a confession. Listening is often your role—whether in oral communications or when you are "listening" to the written word in an exchange of letters.

Chapter 5, "Stories," emphasized that effective listening is an important way of both receiving and sending information. This is particularly true when a loved one confesses his guilt and apologizes for his actions. If you listen to him, you receive information—not only facts about what he has done and plans to do, but also a better understanding of his feelings, fears, hopes, emotional situation, and other information that will help you help him in any of a number of ways. Perhaps more important, when you really listen to a loved one you send a message that you love him, care, value what is being communicated, and respect him. This creates a zone of safety where your loved one can admit his guilt and confess his bad behavior without fear of condemnation or retribution, and begin to see himself as a valuable human being.

Listening requires a conscious effort to hear and take in information. It is more than being quiet and allowing another to talk, or just acknowledging that the other is communicating, or quickly reading a letter without giving its real message much thought. The key is wanting and intending to understand what another is communicating. Good listening requires really trying to understand the meaning of the words and the meaning behind the words. We listen with our ears, mind, eyes, and heart, and begin to see the world as the speaker sees it. We listen to all of what the other person is saying (or writing), become aware of his emotions and feelings. Listening requires us to observe what he is doing, ask questions, offer feedback, encourage him to tell us more, understand his perspective, and accept that his feelings are justified from his perspective.

Some hints for effective listening are:
- Listen to yourself. Your beliefs, biases, and pre-conceived notions of truth often prevent you from listening effectively. Or other things that are going on in your life may distract you, cause you to pay attention to other priorities, or lead to emotions such as anger, sadness, or

frustration that detract from you understanding what is being communicated. These factors become filters that cause you to suit reality to your own needs and wants, and hear what you believe, rather than believe what you hear. To communicate effectively, try to understand the filters through which you listen and make adjustments if they are leading you astray. Critically examine and understand yourself and separate all the distractions from what your loved one is communicating. Acknowledge your differences, control your emotions, and put yourself in your loved one's shoes. You cannot understand that he is different from you, with different feelings, beliefs, and needs, unless you know who you are and acknowledge your own feelings, beliefs, and needs.

- Listen with the right attitude. Your attitude when listening to your loved one (or reading his letters) will strongly influence what you hear, how you interpret the message, how you react—and how he will feel about and respond to you. If you feel put upon, frustrated, angry, or otherwise have a negative attitude, you are almost sure to listen poorly and respond in a way that reflects your attitude. On the other hand, if you have a positive attitude and are interested and engaged, you will hear what he communicates, and will communicate to him that he is valuable and important. To convey a positive attitude, show through your love, patience, and attention that you care about your incarcerated loved one. Stop, look, and listen as though he is the only person in the world. Assume that whatever he is saying is in good faith and try to understand the important ideas being communicated.

- Do not condemn or try to give advice too quickly. When he confesses mistakes, don't condemn him for them, and be slow to give him advice unless it is clearly requested. Doing either will cause you to think too much about your response while your loved one is talking, and may lead to conflict between you. Instead, demonstrate a sincere desire to understand his needs and help him by being quiet and making it obvious that you are listening to him. If advice is in order, it usually can come later.

- Capture the total picture. The great majority of communication is nonverbal, through actions such as tone, body language, expressions, emotions, and even silence. Thus, to effectively listen to your loved one you need to observe him carefully. A key to observing what is being communicated is to look for consistency or inconsistency between what you hear or read and what you see. Look at him, make eye contact, and observe non-verbal as well as verbal communication. Watch the body language and listen to the tone of voice, the rate of speech, the inflection, and particularly changes in these speech characteristics. Look for signs of nervousness, defensiveness, frustration, or anger. Sometimes what you see will be consistent with what you hear, and the two will combine to convey a clear, consistent message. At other times what you see will be inconsistent with what you are hearing, and the message will be garbled. When what you see is inconsistent with what you hear, the non-verbal communication is more likely to be accurate, as people are better able to control what they say than how they look or what they do.

- Offer feedback. Feedback keeps you actively involved in the conversation and tells your loved one his message is being received. Feedback can take several forms. You can use a simple acknowledgment conveyed through encouraging, noncommittal reactions or brief expressions such as "Hum," "Uh-huh," "I see," "Right," "Oh," or "Interesting." You can use non-verbal actions such as head nodding or facial expressions, relaxed and open body movement, eye contact, or touching to show that you are listening. You may wish to summarize or paraphrase what was said (or written) and repeat it back. You may acknowledge the feelings and emotions, or the message behind the message, in what is being communicated. Or you may empathize with your loved one, indicating that you not only perceive his feelings and emotions but also accept them and are able to feel them from her perspective.

- Ask questions. Much of what your loved one says may be incomplete, confusing, vague, inaccurate, or even downright wrong, so asking the right questions at the right time is an important part of listening. Questions not only get information, but also show that you are listening and care enough to seek additional information. Think carefully about when you should ask your questions. Asking too soon is little more than an interruption, and often if you will just wait your question will be answered without being asked. A better approach is usually to observe and listen first, let your loved one have his say, show your interest, and offer other positive feedback before asking questions. Allowing him to "talk it out" helps him lower his emotional level so he can provide more logical and rational answers to your questions when you do ask them. Your letters to him need to have interesting information, but they also need to ask questions—questions that show you care and that will make him think.

Someone once joked, "No man would listen to you talk if he didn't know it was his turn next." Unfortunately, this is too often true. Don't listen so you will have a chance to talk. Listen because you genuinely want information about your loved one, and because you want him to understand that you care. And because listening will encourage confession, which sets the stage for repentance, the topic of the following chapter.

THINGS TO THINK ABOUT

1. WHAT, IF ANYTHING, SHOULD YOU CONFESS TO YOUR LOVED ONE?

2. WHAT CONFESSION WOULD YOU LIKE TO HEAR FROM _____?

3. HOW CAN YOU BE A ROLE MODEL FOR CONFESSION?

4. HOW CAN YOU IMPROVE YOUR LISTENING?

5. I WILL AFFIRM AND ENCOURAGE _____ BY DOING THE FOLLOWING:

9

REPENTANCE

"Change gotta come within each man. Each man's gotta make up his mind."

Think of a time you were on a car trip and became badly lost. You made mistakes along the way, taking wrong turns and following bad directions. You weren't sure where you were, and you didn't know where to go next. Every turn seemed to be the wrong one. The farther you drove, the more lost you became. Then you saw a familiar landmark, and realized you had been going in the wrong direction, directly away from your objective, for a long time. So what did you do? You turned around, made a U-turn, did a "180," took your journey in a new and different direction.

Your bad car trip—a story of mistakes and a U-turn—is a metaphor of a life that has led to prison and the repentance that needs to follow. The offender has been lost, living life in the wrong direction. His behavior has been so contrary to people's expectations and the community's laws that he has been removed from free-world society. To gain peace with society he has to behave differently in the future. But simply making a few changes in his behavior is not enough. He needs to make a U-turn in his life. He needs to make major, fundamental changes that transform who he is. He needs to repent.

A sincerely repentant person hates that aspect of himself that engaged in the hurtful behavior he now regrets. He is remorseful, sorry for what he did—not just sorry that he got caught. Each time he thinks of his bad behavior, he wishes he had made better choices. But repentance involves much more than feeling sorry for one's actions or a change of mind or behavior. It's more than a jailhouse conversion or a temporary change until the problems die down. Repentance is a transformation in which a person's fundamental character and being, not just his surface behavior, become permanently different. It is a process by which humans leave their sins and bad behavior behind and radically and deliberately change their hearts and attitudes as well as their actions.

"When I got locked up for the third time everything came crushing down on me and I knew I had to change. I had destroyed relationships with family and friends. I'd hurt people I didn't know in relation to the crimes I committed. I realized I'd become a monster. That realization set me on a course to change."

Repentance is not a one-time event. It is an ongoing, daily, hourly attitude and change of life for the long term. Richard Owen Roberts, in his book, *Repentance*, explains:

> If someone comes to me with a report about repentance sometime in their past, I want to cry out, "So what? Who cares what happened years ago?" It is never enough to say, "I repented." You must be able to say, "I am repentant. Day in and day out, month after month, year after year, unceasingly, I live as a repentant person. I live in the spirit and attitude of repentance."

Thus, repentance for your loved one requires major change; a movement from where he is, to where he needs to be. He needs to change his mind, heart, and behavior, and become a trouble-free, law-abiding citizen.

UNDERSTANDING EMPATHY

How does one describe the change an incarcerated person needs to make to turn his life around? Perhaps it's easier than you think. Review the discussion in Chapter 3 on causes of crime. One common thread runs through those causes; the single characteristic that seems to drive so much criminal behavior?

It's that most offenders have been living a "me-centered" life. Think about whether your loved one has fit this pattern. Have you seen a focus on "me" play out in one or more of the following ways?

- Thinking and acting from his own perspective and not considering other people's
- Meeting his own needs and wants while disregarding those of others
- Abusing his power and control regardless of the feelings or welfare of others
- Demanding "respect" by using threats and fear rather than earning true respect
- Letting anger control him without regard to the feelings of others
- Feeding his addictions no matter what the consequences for others—or himself
- Considering himself rather than those he has hurt as the real victim
- Other behavior patterns suggesting he thinks first of himself and disregards others

"Like many young people out there today. I was born with a hard head, lived by my own rules. My greed and pride kept me beleiving couldn't be had and that I didn't need God."

Has his life focused on "me" to such an extent that he violated the law to benefit himself and failed to consider the legitimate needs, concerns, and feelings of others? If so, he lacks empathy. Empathy is understanding, being aware of, being sensitive to, and vicariously experiencing the feelings, thoughts, and experience of another. Empathy is walking a mile in another person's sandals. It is probably the most fundamental characteristic for putting the "me" focus behind and sincerely repenting.

Being empathetic requires your incarcerated loved one to move into other persons' worlds with understanding and feeling. It goes beyond an objective understanding of what he's done, how he hurt other people, and where he needs to be. Empathy puts understanding into his heart and soul and allows him to feel the remorse that is necessary for true repentance. If your loved one truly feels what others—you, your family, his victim(s), and others—feel, he will want to change. And if he wants to change, he can and will change.

People often confuse empathy with sympathy. With sympathy, you feel for another. You're sorry for them, or feel pity for them, or are concerned about them. But you don't feel what they feel, because you don't walk in their shoes. With empathy, you feel *with* another person rather than *for* him. You feel his feelings.

Research suggests that empathy is a key, if not the key, to all human social interaction and morality. It is considered by many a fundamental necessity for an inmate to turn his life around and avoid re-offending. Without empathy, there would be no reason for him to quit a life of crime—except for his own self-interest of avoiding punishment, which rarely works.

"I have realized that I have hurt you and you have lost loved ones that will never be replaced. I know you have or had anger and revenge in your mind. I also lost a brother to a criminal and was full of hatred and was thirsty for a bloody revenge but my thought aren't god's thought he put forgiveness in my heart."

Empathy requires imagination, work, and possibly even a similar experience. It is difficult to be fully empathetic, because one's reactions, thoughts, and feelings in a particular circumstance may be different from others'. But to transform his life, your loved one needs to empathize with the people he has hurt and with those he might hurt. He needs to walk in the shoes of his direct victim(s), of you, of his entire family, close friends, and others.

HELPING YOUR LOVED ONE DEVELOP EMPATHY

Childhood, as early as infancy, is a critical time for the development of empathy, and feelings and attitudes developed as a child are difficult to change. But your loved one can become more empathetic. And you can support him in the process.

How do you help your loved one develop empathy, and transform his life from me-centered to other-centered? Let's start with some strategies that don't work:

- Shame: pointing out how dumb his life has been, or trying to make him feel bad for his many mistakes, or questioning his value as a person
- Threats: warning about the bad things you will do if he continues in his current lifestyle
- Condemnation: putting him down or making fun of him, particularly in front of others
- Criticism: harping on his faults, no matter how small they may be
- Cynicism: questioning his motives or claiming he is selfish

These strategies may—possibly—lead to a form of change. But at best the change probably will be temporary rather than long term, a change of current behavior rather than of mind and heart, a short smooth spot in the road rather than a U-turn in your loved one's life. More likely, these strategies will lead to anger, alienation, and a continued focus on "me."

Some strategies that will help him develop empathy are discussed below.

Be a Role Model of Empathy

Being a role model for your loved one will require you to empathize with him, when it's probably easier to feel sorry for him, or pity him, or feel concern about him. So empathizing with your loved one may require some work. You have to be careful to not allow empathy for him to appear to justify his crime or to absolve him from responsibility for its consequences. The following will help:

- Be confident. Like yourself enough to be patient, kind and ready to admit when you are wrong. Accepting yourself as you are will help you see him as he is.
- Challenge your prejudices. We all have assumptions about others and use collective labels—especially for inmates—that prevent us from appreciating their individuality and value as human beings. This is often true even for those we love. Challenge your preconceptions and prejudices by searching for ways you and your loved one are alike rather than different. You probably will find you are more alike than you thought.
- Connect with him. Discuss his situation with him. Don't interrogate him, but do ask pertinent questions. Understand his life and world view. Don't just chat about the weather, family, or friends. Ask how he is doing, and mean it. Get serious, and try to understand the world in his head—his day to day existence, his problems and difficulties, his loneliness and other feelings, what gives him hope, his faith. Discuss his emotional and mental state and help him understand how feelings, desires, and emotions can influence behavior. Pray with him if he is willing.

> *"I have decided to make a more permanent change in my life and plan to remove all the hate, anger and bitterness I have been living with for the last 45 years. I'm tired of hurting inside and have decided that only God and Jesus can give me peace of mind."*

- Treat him as you want to be treated. Acknowledge the difficulty of his situation without claiming to understand it. Respect him as an individual human being with a mind of his own, without endorsing his past behavior. Work on

your relationship. Acknowledge his difficulties and how you may have contributed to them, apologize if appropriate, or simply tell him you want to bring more empathy and compassion (and less judgment, advice, self-righteousness, etc.) to your relationship.
- Listen to him. Review Chapter 8 for thoughts on doing so.

Encourage Him in His Faith

Chapter 4, "Faith," noted that the Christian faith provides a great moral code, emphasizes love and hope, and lays out a process for change. Another important teaching of Christianity, as well as most of the world's other major religions, is its emphasis on empathy.

The word "empathy" does not appear in the Bible, but biblical teaching includes compassion, loving others as self, listening, and other lessons that are at the core of empathy. For example, Job 2:11-13 clearly describes empathy when it tells of three of Job's friends who heard of Job's suffering and "decided to go and comfort him." When they recognized him, "they began to weep and wail, tearing their clothes in grief and throwing dust into the air and on their heads. Then they sat there on the ground with him for seven days and nights without saying a word, because they saw how much he was suffering." And in Romans 12:15 the apostle Paul exhorted fellow Christians to "Be happy with those who are happy, weep with those who weep." And perhaps it's all covered in Matthew 7:12, typically called the Golden Rule, "Do for others what you want them to do for you." Each of these scriptures, and many others, contemplates feeling what others feel, walking in their sandals.

Thus, learning about the Christian faith and reading the Bible can foster empathy. But how do you get your loved one to buy in? The best way is to demonstrate Jesus' charge in Matthew 22:34-40 to love your neighbor as yourself; and in Matthew 5:43-44 to love your enemies and pray for those who persecute you.

Following this guidance demonstrates a message of love that is unconditional, foundational, and unshakeable—given completely and without reservation. When you demonstrate such love, you teach empathy.

At the risk of repeating too much of Chapter 4, become a witness of Christ through the natural outcome of living for Him. Pray, for yourself, for your loved one, and for your family. Pray together with your loved one if he is willing. Give him a Bible. Read the Bible and live by its moral code, and read it with him if he is willing. Talk about your empathetic feelings toward a victim you both know of. Write about your faith in your letters and offer to attend church together after his release, always being sensitive to where each of you is during your faith journey and to the potential dangers of overt evangelizing. Walk in his shoes, and see your efforts to support his faith as he sees them.

"It took me a little over a year to complete the Bible and it still amazes me to this day how the stories in the Bible helped comfort me at different points in prison, it was God comforting me. God was knocking on my heart, but I didn't know it."

Encourage Him to Participate in Restorative Justice Programs

Most prisons make available a number of religious programs offered by faith groups. As noted above, most religions foster empathy, so attending prison religious services should help your loved one to become more empathic with others. Encourage him to participate in these services.

"Until taking this class I never gave it a lot of thought about the impact crime has on society as a whole. I have now sence been shown the devestation it causes first hand. And it's not a pretty sight."

Restorative justice, deeply rooted in all the world's major religions, focuses on the harm crime does to people and communities, offender accountability, and affected parties working together to find solutions. These principles imply an inherent concern for victims, their injuries, and their need to regain control over their lives and have their rights vindicated. Those responsible for harms are expected to repair the damage they have caused and address the underlying causes to the extent possible. This focus on victims and mutual solutions is, at its core, empathy. An offender cannot really be concerned with victims unless he feels what they feel, walks in their sandals. Unless he empathizes with them.

Restorative justice programs are available in a number of prisons. They tend to focus on victim awareness, victim-offender dialogue, and preparing offenders for release.

Tell your loved one about the presence of restorative justice programs generally, and encourage him to volunteer to participate if one is available at his unit. In most cases he should contact his unit chaplain for assistance in understanding what is available and signing up if appropriate.

Bridges To Life, discussed in the "Introduction" and the model for this book, is a faith-based restorative justice program with a strong victim focus. Throughout its fourteen-week program, victims tell their stories to inmates: stories that are very personal accounts of the effects of crime and the pain of living with them every day. Small groups of inmates discuss the stories and the effect of their crimes, and they, slowly, incrementally, but surely, develop a sense of empathy for those they have hurt.

"Since taking this program, I have learned many things about myself, and life in general. It has opened my 'eyes' and 'heart' in new ways I've never seen or felt before. For this I am forever greatful."

Bridges To Life is available in many Texas prisons and some in other states. If a BTL program is not available, use www.bridgestolife.org to have a copy of *Restoring Peace*, the centerpiece of the BTL curriculum, sent to your loved one for his personal reading.

THINGS TO THINK ABOUT

1. DO YOU BELIEVE YOUR LOVED ONE NEEDS TO MAKE A U-TURN IN HIS LIFE? WHY OR WHY NOT?

2. HAVE YOU USED SHAME, CONDEMNATION, THREATS, CRITICISM, OR CYNICISM IN YOUR RELATIONSHIP WITH _____? HOW DID IT WORK?

3. WITH WHOM SHOULD _____ FEEL EMPATHY IF HE IS TO DO A U-TURN IN HIS LIFE?

4. LIST THREE THINGS YOU CAN DO TO BE A ROLE MODEL OF EMPATHY FOR _____.

5. LIST THREE ADDITIONAL THINGS YOU CAN DO TO ENCOURAGE _____ TO EMPATHIZE WITH OTHERS.

10

FORGIVENESS

"I had a problem asking people to forgive me and I still have a slight problem because of all the bad things I've done. But I'm really and truly sorry, and I ask for your forgiveness."

The Old Testament tells of Manasseh, who became king of Judah when he was twelve years old and reigned for fifty-five years. He was one of the most evil of all kings. Manasseh consulted spirit-mediums, fortune tellers, and sorcerers; encouraged his people to worship heathen idols; and rebuilt heathen altars for worshipping the sun, moon, and stars in the very place where the Lord had said He would be honored forever. Manasseh sacrificed his own children as burnt offerings, and tradition has it that he gave the order to have Isaiah the prophet sawn in two. He was personally evil, and seduced Judah and the inhabitants of Jerusalem to do even more evil.

After Manasseh was defeated in battle and taken prisoner he cried out to God for help, humbling himself and asking for mercy and grace. "And the Lord listened, and answered his plea by returning him to Jerusalem and to his kingdom! At that point Manasseh finally realized that the Lord was really God." (2 Chronicles 33: 1-13) Manasseh, among the most evil of all kings, asked for forgiveness and God forgave him. This example of bad deeds being forgiven sets the stage for this chapter.

Forgiveness is granting pardon or giving up resentment for a harm or debt. It involves looking back at what happened, but not for the purpose of analyzing, blaming, or condemning. Forgiveness looks back for the purpose of leaving the offense behind and moving on to a better future. It does not forget the past or change the bad things that have happened. But it does change the present and can change the future.

"I pray that the creator will continue to bless you with happiness, love and pace. I pray he will give you the strength to forgive me & restore your faith in your fellow human beings."

Forgiveness involves more than just getting beyond guilt. It is not just a formula, or saying "I forgive you," or a single action taken to make things seem better. Importantly:

- Forgiveness does not condone bad behavior. When you forgive someone, you are not saying that what he did was right. You let him off the hook of any emotional obligation to you for what has happened, but you do not endorse what he did or say doing it again is acceptable.
- Forgiveness does not mean forgetting. That Texas philosopher, Willie Nelson, had it at least partly right when he sang, "Forgiving is easy, but forgetting takes a long time." Forgiving isn't always easy, but it does not mean we forget. It is getting beyond, not forgetting, denying, or minimizing.
- Forgiveness is not the same as mercy. It does not mean the offender should not pay the consequences. As we discussed in the chapters on responsibility and accountability, offenders need to deal with the effects of their actions and answer for what they have done.

Instead, true forgiveness is a journey involving confession, repentance, and love of enemies. It gets beyond hurt and includes a commitment to a way of life in which people seek reconciliation and fellowship with God and others. Without the journey, "forgiveness" may help a person feel better, or get beyond hate, or even improve his behavior. But it does not restore fellowship with God and others.

"I want you to know I am taking full responsibility for my actions."

Forgiveness allows us to overcome intense negative feelings such as resentment, anger, hatred, and desire for revenge. It allows us to take our hurt less personally, and take responsibility for how we feel. Forgiveness increases our positive emotions such as hope, care, affection, trust, and happiness; helps develop a better spiritual view; and helps with our healing. It sets the stage for restoring or improving our relationships. And it can even contribute to our physical health.

Sometimes we need to ask for forgiveness, and sometimes we need to grant it. And forgiveness is a choice. You and I do not have to forgive anyone who has offended us, and people we have offended do not have to forgive us. No one can force us to change our mind and heart, no one can force us to forgive or ask for forgiveness or accept forgiveness, and no one can prevent us from forgiving.

The sections that follow will help you think about forgiving your loved one, and also consider how you can help him with his own forgiveness issues.

FORGIVING YOUR LOVED ONE

Your loved one has hurt you—probably time and again, by his behavior before prison and certainly by being convicted and sent to prison. He may have done you more harm than your worst enemy. He may not seem to deserve forgiveness, and forgiving him may be difficult.

"I've hurt my family and my bad decisions have led friends and loved ones to sever ties with me. There's a guilt and shame that manifests from all the bad choices I've made. At one point in my life I allowed the guilt and shame to consume me—today it's a constant battle because that type of guilt and shame works to steal a person's hope. When I was overcome with guilt and shame I felt defeated—defeated to the point of giving up on things positive."

Some hurts are so bad they cannot be minimized in any way, and forgiving them will always be difficult. Even thinking about forgiving what happened in some situations may seem to trivialize them. To help deal with the difficulty, remember that forgiving does not require you to look the other way, act as if no wrong has been committed, excuse the inexcusable, tolerate the intolerable, or sweep things under the rug. Forgiveness just requires you to get beyond them.

When you have been badly hurt, you can decide that you will forgive your loved one, and let time help you actually do so. You may have to hurt enough to want to forgive, and go through an "acceptance time" during which your mind and heart learn to live with what has happened and the hatred and resentment gradually subside.

Other hurts are not so bad and may be easier to forgive when placed in the right context. Think about all the surrounding circumstances when you were hurt, as this may lead to a conclusion that the offense was not as bad as you thought. You may conclude that although the offense(s) is not excusable, it is understandable under all the circumstances. If you remind yourself that you are just one among many who have suffered a similar offense, it may seem less significant. In many cases the one who hurt you did not intend to hurt you personally, and refusing to see an offense as a personal attack makes forgiving it easier.

Your forgiveness should be unconditional. Recall the story of the prodigal son, discussed in Chapter 8. The father welcomed his son home as soon as he saw him on the horizon, before he knew whether or not he would confess and repent. His son's attitude didn't matter. He was forgiven.

Sometimes your loved one loved one will be remorseful, and will confess, repent, and perhaps even ask for forgiveness. If this happens, go full bore. Forgive him in your heart. Tell him you forgive him. Tell him you love him. Work to improve your fellowship with him.

"You both are and have always been special to me and I also want you to know that it's hurt me deeply not being able to be here for you. I'm sure it might not be easy for you to forgive me, but I ask that you do forgive me."

But what if your loved one is not remorseful and repentant, or perhaps isn't interested in your forgiveness? Sometimes telling an unrepentant person you forgive him will be misinterpreted and understood to mean you think his behavior was okay—and he has permission to continue it. Sometimes if the person is in denial telling him you forgive him can be construed as arrogant and too judgmental, and the person will resent it rather than accept it.

In such situations, you can welcome confession and repentance from him if and when it occurs, but you cannot force your loved one to do what you think he should do. If you insist he take these actions before you forgive him, you are giving your loved one the power to control whether and when you forgive. This allows him to hurt you twice: once in the original offense and again when he refuses to allow you the healing you could obtain by forgiving him.

Deal with these concerns by treating forgiveness as a journey with a number of milestones. Start the journey by forgiving him in your heart, loving him without reservation, and working to establish or improve your fellowship with him—all without confronting him or telling him you forgive him. Circumstances are likely to improve. Then, when you feel the time is right, you can tell him you forgive him. You will know the right time if you approach the decision with love and with his long-term best interest in your heart. And remember that it may take time and persistence. When Jesus was asked how many times we should forgive, he answered "seventy times seven," which seems to mean there is no end to our need to forgive. (Matthew 18:22)

HELPING YOUR LOVED ONE FORGIVE HIMSELF

The greatest wish of many inmates, and perhaps your loved one, is to be able to "forgive myself." Many are filled with guilt, shame, and self-loathing at the lives they've lived and the crimes they've committed. They feel so bad because they have failed to meet their own expectations of themselves and have done a continuing string of things—criminal or not—that have hurt others and that they know are wrong and shameful. They live with hopelessness. They frequently say that they just cannot forgive themselves.

"It breaks my heart knowing the reason I went to your house was to get some new syringes so I could shoot more dope. You knew it and you told me you loved me. I wish I could make it up to you but I can't. From what I've been told I was the last person to see you alive. I don't think I can ever forgive myself. The closest I can come to making this up to you is a living amends. I have finally sobered up that's a start."

Can offenders really forgive themselves? Does anyone have the right or authority to forgive himself for hurting others? Reasonable people might disagree. However, both the Old and New Testaments describe a God who loves the unlovable; a God of grace and merciful forgiveness. It is a forgiven-ness based on grace, albeit one that requires and enables repentance that acknowledges the individual's particular sin and crime. Unless your loved one's standards are higher than God's, he can accept God's forgiveness. Said differently, he can forgive himself.

Nevertheless, self-forgiveness is often difficult for an offender wallowing in the shame of his misguided life. While self-forgiveness is something he has to do himself, you can help him during your visits, by phone, or by letter.

- Encourage him to live a repentant life as discussed in Chapter 9. Self-forgiveness without a commitment to change is a sign of nothing more than moral shallowness.

- Tell your loved one you forgive him. Having a loved one forgive him makes self-forgiveness seem more reasonable.
- Discuss God's forgiveness with him.
- Encourage the view that no one is perfect. We all make mistakes and bad decisions. He needs to join the human race, where we all fail at some things and sometimes hurt other people. Every mistake he has made probably has been made thousands of times by other people. All of us need forgiveness.
- Remind him that forgiving himself does not mean he is condoning what he has done. It's still wrong. He's just allowing himself to get beyond it.
- Encourage him to acknowledge his forgiveness. He can look in the mirror every morning and tell himself he is a child of God, God has forgiven him, and it's okay that he has forgiven himself.

This is the easy part. Now we move to forgiveness from others—those your loved one has hurt.

HELPING YOUR LOVED ONE ASK FOR FORGIVENESS

If your loved one is remorseful and repentant, he will want to be forgiven by those he has hurt—his direct victims, their families, you, your extended family, and others. Being forgiven by others is part of his healing process. It shows him there is sufficient goodness in him that someone else has judged him forgivable, and allows him to begin to find peace. But he needs to do his part if he hopes for others to forgive him.

In previous chapters we have discussed the importance of his taking responsibility, being accountable, confessing, and leading a repentant life as pre-requisites to forgiveness. That will not be repeated here. Let's talk here about the simple act of his asking for forgiveness.

"There may still be an amount of shame, anger, disappointment, and even bitterness that you're experiencing. I accept it, cause so do I. Yet, all is left for us now is to use the time God is giving us. To grow through these emotions and events of the past & present that we can be "better not bitter." As I've ask before, I'll ask again and do my best with Gods guidance to demonstrate forgiveness in my daily actions. 'Please forgive me?' by accepting my apologies, allowing us the opportunity to walk lifes journey in Gods grace and peace together ...

Love,

Daddy"

Asking forgiveness from others while your loved one is locked in prison will be difficult at best, sometimes impossible. Opportunities for communication will be limited. Contact with some victims is probably prohibited. But where contact is feasible, you can encourage him to seek forgiveness. If you do, empathize with his situation and help him understand the following:

- Forgiving him may be very difficult for those he has hurt. They are likely to require time and effort. He needs to empathize with them, feel their pain, and think how difficult his hurt must have been for them. Even asking for forgiveness might be considered an arrogant insult. This means he needs to seriously consider whether, and when, to ask for forgiveness.
- Forgiving him is the other person's choice, and there is no way your loved one can force it. The other person may be unwilling, at least at the time, to move beyond his anger, resentment, and other vindictive passions. The other person will determine whether and when he will forgive your loved one.

- Asking for forgiveness is asking someone to do something important. Your loved one needs to ask with humility and respect, because granting forgiveness is the other person's gift to him.
- Your loved one can do everything right and still those he has hurt will not tell him they forgive him. If this happens, he needs to empathize with them, remember that forgiveness is a process and over time they may forgive him, and remember that God will still forgive him.
- He needs to remember the power of asking for forgiveness. Just asking for forgiveness is the sincerest form of confession, and it often leads to new hope, a fresh start, a new beginning.

"It's not easy being away from yal, and not being able to see yal everyday. I'll give anything except my soul just to be able to hold yal in my arms even for a few minutes. ... The special events and yal life I should had been there. I know I'm not the only one doing time. We all are but I want yal to keep pushing Forward Trust God, and His Son Jesus Christ. I'm Proud of all yal and love yal. Please Forgive me, for being away from yal at such a Special time and yal lives."

A final thought: As noted above, sometimes actually asking a victim for forgiveness is impossible. But your loved one can still ask for forgiveness. Encourage him to write a long letter repenting and asking for forgiveness, and file it away without sending it. Or send it to a surrogate, perhaps you. This is not perfect, but it will bring some of the peace of personally asking for forgiveness.

HELPING YOUR LOVED ONE FORGIVE OTHERS

For most offenders, forgiving others raises significant and highly personal issues. Many offenders, especially those who are women, are themselves victims of bad behavior or crime. They may have been seriously abused, neglected, or trained in their criminal ways by others who should have loved them. It's difficult to forgive a father who left home, returned periodically to degrade and beat him and his mother, and is still engaged in a life of women, drink, and drugs. Or a step-father who sexually abused her—or, more often than we like to believe, him—for years. Or a "friend" who lied to him and led him down the wrong path. Your loved one may be angry, resentful, or bitter about what has been done to him, and reluctant to forgive.

So—what are you to do? How can you help your loved one deal with his anger and forgive those who have hurt him? Consider the following:

- Don't claim you "understand." You probably don't, particularly if you haven't been there. But you can say "I hear you" and "I'm sorry." You can empathize with your loved one.
- Don't try to pressure your loved one to forgive someone who has victimized her or him. A hollow forgiveness in the face of real anger and bitterness leads, not to reconciliation and a new life, but to repressed bitterness and worse hatred. Even suggesting forgiveness may tend to discount your loved one's valid feeling of anger, hatred, and desire for revenge. Encouraging your loved one to forgive too easily seems to blame her for suffering, to add insult to injury by making her feel guilty or ashamed over a reaction that under the circumstances is natural, fitting, and proper.
- Remember that forgiveness of any significance cannot just be willed and rarely happens overnight. How long it takes will depend on the relationship of the people involved, whether the hurt was deliberate or accidental, the magnitude of the damage, whether it was a one-time event or a continuing problem, and other such factors. Sometimes people have to hurt enough to want to forgive. They have to go through an "acceptance time" during which the mind

and heart learn to live with what has happened and the hatred and resentment gradually subside. They also have to think about the idea of forgiveness and the event(s) long enough that they can make it part of their story and begin to put some "ignored" puzzle pieces together.
- Help your loved one put his hatred into context: to be truthful about what happened, to see that it has also happened to others, to recognize that notwithstanding his hurt he has voluntarily made the choices that put him where he is, and that he is subject to God's forgiving and reconciling love.
- Focus on your loved one's needs, not on your own need to preach a particular view of forgiveness. If your loved one is not yet prepared to forgive, focus on loving him and leave the specific question of forgiveness to God, who is better able to handle it.

A good test of whether there has been real forgiveness is whether those involved are moving toward reconciliation. More about that in the following chapter.

THINGS TO THINK ABOUT

1. HAVE YOU FORGIVEN _____? SHOULD YOU? WHEN AND HOW WILL YOU FORGIVE HIM?

2. IS _____ STRUGGLING WITH FORGIVING HIMSELF? HAVE YOU DISCUSSED THIS WITH HIM? SHOULD YOU?

3. LIST THREE PEOPLE YOU BELIEVE _____ SHOULD ASK TO FORGIVE HIM? ARE YOU COMFORTABLE DISCUSSING THIS WITH HIM? IF SO, HOW SHOULD YOU GO ABOUT IT?

4. LIST THREE PEOPLE YOU BELIEVE _____ SHOULD FORGIVE. ARE YOU COMFORTABLE DISCUSSING THIS WITH HIM? IF SO, HOW SHOULD YOU GO ABOUT IT?

5. ARE YOU ONE OF THE PEOPLE _____ NEEDS TO FORGIVE? HOW WILL YOU HANDLE THIS SITUATION?

11

RECONCILIATION

"The only thing I can do is ask for your forgiveness and let you know if there is any amends or way to reconcile to you individually, please tell me."

Imagine that your loved one is incarcerated in one of the "old style" prisons constructed one hundred plus years ago, featuring a high brick wall around its perimeter. The "Walls" unit in Huntsville, Texas is a good example. Constructed in the 1840s, its perimeter is a thirty-foot-high, red brick wall. Offenders on the inside cannot go over it, or around it, or through it to get out. Nor can families on the outside get in as they desire. It's a wall of separation that, physically, keeps people separated from their loved ones.

Unfortunately, walls often also separate you emotionally and spiritually from your loved one, and perhaps from others you probably should have a relationship with. They are walls that prevent the connection and closeness that all of us probably yearn for.

"When a person is incarcerated the context of all their relationships change. What has always been their most important relationships, with family, loved ones, and friends, become distant and limited due to the separation, and also to the bad decisions that affected family and friends. I've hurt my family and my bad decisions have led friends & loved ones to sever ties with me."

Fortunately, however, you can tear down the wall of separation. You can't blast it down with one big charge. But just as one could slowly, gradually break the mortar and remove one brick at a time until a brick wall is down, you can slowly, over time, "one brick at a time," take down the emotional and spiritual wall separating you from your loved one. This journey of tearing down the wall of separation is called reconciliation.

Reconciliation is different in different situations. A person with internal conflicts might reconcile within himself. Another person might reconcile with God. But we most often think of people reconciling with one another. This coming together of two (or perhaps more) people is the way we will consider reconciliation here: people who have a wall of separation between them tearing it down and creating a healthy, mutually satisfying relationship. It is the important next step in the journey toward peace.

Building and maintaining a satisfying relationship with your incarcerated loved one (You may not consider him a "loved one" at the present time, but that's the way he will be referred to here.) is important for both of you. It will give him a feeling of connectedness and communion that minimizes his sense of isolation and loneliness, makes his sentence somewhat less intolerable, and sets the stage for a more supportive community after his release. And it will give you the satisfaction of knowing that you are making a genuine effort to maintain your relationships and the integrity of your family and community—currently and for the future.

DECIDING WHEN RECONCILIATION IS NEEDED

Reconciling is a personal choice for you and your loved one. But you probably need to consider reconciling if you are estranged: if you, and perhaps your loved one, have been so damaged, or neglected, or misled, or disappointed, or otherwise hurt that you have no contact at all. If you do not reconcile, the uncertainty, resentment, fear, anger, hatred, desire for revenge, and other bad feelings that each of you probably is carrying will be with you forever.

"I sense a huge dark cloud of failure that looms over me constantly. Alienation from family and friends. On one sentence I spent ten years and I only had two visits from my

family during those ten years. That for sure was a problem."

You and your loved one may also need to reconcile even if you are not estranged: if your relationship is not as healthy or mutually satisfying as it should be, and you (and probably your loved one as well) would like to improve it. You may want to reconcile if one or both engage in behaviors such as the following:

- Place conditions on your love. He seems to love you only if you do what he wants. You show your love only when he straightens up and flies right.
- Are not open and honest. You withhold information or lie about what is going on at home, perhaps refusing to discuss bad situations in order to "protect" him. He lies when he tells you he is okay but isn't, or that he stays away from contraband drugs and reads his Bible daily. Both of you fail to address the "pink elephant" in the room: that huge problem everyone knows about but is unwilling to acknowledge or discuss.
- Engage in emotional abuse and manipulation. He puts you down or makes you feel guilty because you don't visit enough, or put enough money in his account, or do things he doesn't like. You put him down because of the life he has led, or his difficulties dealing with prison life.
- Attempt to use coercion and threats. You withhold, or threaten to withhold, visits or letters as punishment in order to get him to act as you want. He uses relationships with others to drive a wedge between the two of you.
- Engage in minimizing, denying, and/or blaming. He refuses to acknowledge or makes light of the difficulties you are encountering, or refuses to accept any responsibility for what you are dealing with in the real world, such as raising his children, paying all the bills, and keeping a home going when he's not there. You make light of his situation and claim it isn't as bad as he says.

- Use family and loved ones. You make him feel guilty because he isn't helping with the children, or you threaten not to bring them to visitation. He tries to manipulate the children to hurt you.
- Focus on resentment rather than forgiveness. You just can't forgive him for what he has done. He just can't forgive you for what you have done, or for what he perceives you have done.
- Build your relationship on fantasy. Each of you pretends you have a good relationship when you know you really don't. Or you completely live in the past without focusing on your needs or theirs in the present situation. You smile and pretend.

If your relationship with a loved one is characterized by one or several of these problems, you probably want to develop a more satisfying one.

FINDING A MUTUALLY SATISFYING RELATIONSHIP

The goal in reconciling is to develop a relationship that is as mutually satisfying as is feasible under the circumstances. A mutually satisfying relationship is one that acknowledges and addresses "his" needs, "my" needs, and "our" needs. There is not a giver and a taker. Instead, all give and all take. Each person's thoughts, feelings, and actions are appropriately responsive to the other's.

This doesn't necessarily mean developing a close relationship or returning to what was there in the past. Some behavior is so hurtful or has affected you so badly that a close or continuing relationship with the perpetrator may not be possible or appropriate. For example, an abusive or exploitative relationship should not be recreated. Or sometimes attempts to fix an intimate relationship that just wouldn't work may be doomed to failure. Instead, both parties can strive to make the relationship as satisfying as possible, with boundaries appropriate for the circumstances.

"When we first met we were happy for about a year and then the arguing started, but not anymore. I need you to understand that I am going to make more permanent changes ..."

While no single, right relationship is best in all situations, one that includes the following characteristics will likely be as good as it can be:

- Is built on honesty and trust. Each of you is open and honest. You tell the truth, do what you say you will do, and each can depend on the other. You are willing to discuss the "pink elephant" in the room.

    "I can even accept you all writing telling me you all do not want anything to do with me. I could then know what I need to do with the way I feel. I would know what is up with you all."

- You are friends and you treat each other as friends who respect one another. You do not condemn one another, you value each other's opinions, and you attempt to understand and affirm the other's emotions. Your friendship has staying power. You stick together through good times and bad.

- Each of you is willing to be vulnerable. You are willing to take the risk of opening yourself to the other, being completely honest, asking for what you want, being generous in your response to the other's needs, and demonstrating your love.

- You feel safe with one another. Each of you tries to meet the security needs of the other before meeting your own. You provide reassurance with reliable, consistent behavior. Each of you focuses on the other, and is totally selfless.

- Each of you is willing to sacrifice, without feeling you are making a sacrifice. It's one thing to maintain a relationship when the going is easy. Can you still do so while you are in the midst of all the sacrifices and problems caused by his incarceration?
- Both of you have boundaries. Each can say "no" to requests or tell the other when something doesn't feel right, without feeling guilty.
- Each of you listens loud, as discussed in Chapter 8.
- Both of you are working on your relationship. You visit, write, email, or call as often as feasible and appropriate within the boundaries of your relationship. And each of you makes his or her best effort to build a relationship with as many of these characteristics as possible.

A mutually satisfying relationship starts with small improvements, adapts to new situations, and grows over time. It is likely to change continuously. And it includes as many of these characteristics as possible. If you don't continually work on it, a satisfactory relationship is likely to gradually deteriorate, and you will drift further apart—emotionally, if not physically. Good relationships require management, effort, and attention.

RECONCILING

Reconciling is a choice for you and your loved one. What it looks like will vary, depending on the circumstances. Your human frailties will often make it very difficult. You are an imperfect human and so is he. And the time may or may not be right; the stage may or may not be set. Look closely at your situation and make conscious decisions about what to do.

Decide if the Time is Right

Reconciliation between a free person and an incarcerated person presents some unique problems. Your incarcerated loved one is locked up, probably lonely and yearning for almost any contact with a family member, lover, or just about anyone from the outside world. He may want—perhaps need—reconciliation more than you do. But his ability to do anything about it is limited. You may, probably do, have problems of your own. You are free, and have more opportunities to get on with your life generally as you see fit. You are more able to take the initiative in the matter of your relationship. In sum, there is a power imbalance. Whether there is reconciliation, and what it looks like, is probably largely up to you. This places on you an extra burden of being fair.

"And while I strive daily to become the Word as it is written in St. Matthew, chapters five, six, and seven, one of my greatest desires is to share that Word with my father before it is too late and time runs out on life."

When considering reconciliation under these circumstances, look first at yourself and your role in any conflict with your loved one. It's easy to blame him, and he may well be primarily responsible for the breakdown of your relationship. But you may have some responsibility as well, and you can only control your own behavior. Therefore, start your consideration of reconciling by focusing on yourself. Ask yourself questions such as:

- Has enough time passed since the conflict or estrangement that I can reflect carefully, objectively, and honestly on our situation and look at the big picture?
- Why did the conflict happen? Who is responsible for what? Can I accept responsibility for any part that I played?
- In what ways am I accountable to the other person? Can I acknowledge that accountability?
- If I have been part of the problem, have I repented and committed to change? If not, is long-term reconciliation or an improved relationship possible?

Next, consider the situation and desires of your loved one. His view of the situation between you is probably very different from yours. Some level of conflict may exist and he may be highly emotional, filled with anger, bitterness, jealousy, sadness, or some other feeling that may make reconciliation difficult or seemingly impossible. Look carefully and objectively at him and think about whether he wants an honest, sincere reconciliation or just some regular mail and visits. Is he still too angry or too hurt or too bitter to reconcile at the emotional level? Think about the previous chapters of this book. How has he handled responsibility, accountability, confession, repentance, and forgiveness? Does he need more time to adjust to the situation and make reconciliation possible? You can always be surprised, but usually you won't be. If you listen, empathize, and care deeply about your loved one's situation you can probably decide whether he is now capable of reconciling.

"My family means so much to me. When I do not hear from you all, I worry, stress, stay angery and the things I am doing to better myself seem empty. I feel empty and like nothing I do is worth the time."

Honestly answering such questions about yourself and your loved one should tell you whether the time is right for you to attempt to mend your relationship with him. Without positive answers, trying to do so may appear to work at first but will probably lead to eventual frustration and further conflict.

Think About the Type of Relationship to Seek

If you conclude the time is right to try to reconcile, you will need to seek a mutually advantageous relationship. But what does this look like? How do you address both of your interests? A relationship is not likely to last or be productive if one person wins and the other loses. Reconciliation is about building relationships, not getting your way. Both people need to feel a sense of fairness, even if the issues between you are not always resolved.

What will be mutually satisfying will be different, depending on the circumstances. Has the hurt been so great that a relationship like you had in the past is not possible or appropriate? Will your loved one be locked up for two years—or a lifetime? Is this is his first rodeo or his fourth time in the big house? Should the two of you just try to quit fighting and let bygones be bygones, or seek a business-like relationship, or be friends, or become lovers? Your loved one may not agree, and may want a different kind of relationship than you want. Remember that reconciliation is a journey, not an event, and you probably need to start small and allow your relationship to grow. Perhaps you first talk civilly, then become friends, then allow your relationship to grow as both of you think it should. Let your mutual efforts to reconcile shed light on what your new relationship should be.

If now is the time to go forward, consider the thoughts outlined in the following sections.

Build an Environment for Reconciliation

For reasons discussed above, you will probably need to take the lead if reconciliation is possibly in your future. But trying to force reconciliation when one or both of you are not ready could lead instead to further conflict, estrangement, and anger—and make your lives more miserable. Your best bet is to start by creating an environment that is conducive to discernment and good decisions in your mutual best interests.

Start by praying for your loved one. Praying for him brings him into your heart, helps you empathize with him, begins to break down any hostility and distinction between the two of you, and starts to develop or strengthen a "friendship." Also pray for discernment in the road ahead. Praying for God's help will help give you the courage to attempt what can be a difficult and risky endeavor. God will guide your efforts.

"I know you are wondering about my daughter and there has been no appovement. I only talked to her that one time and have not recived any mail from her. But as you had told me you have to do your part and let God do the rest and that is what I am doing!"

Find opportunities to build trust. Trust is the unwritten and usually unspoken contract that allows people to believe in the honesty, integrity, reliability, and justice of one another. It is an essential ingredient for reconciliation. Building trust if you have no contact is impossible. But if you are communicating within an existing but bad relationship, or can establish some level of communication to end an estrangement, you have the foundation for learning to trust one another.

Trust has many dimensions, none more important than honesty. The most important thing you can do to foster mutual trust is to be honest, whether that term means being truthful in a general sense, doing what you say you will do, calling a spade a spade, being willing to confess and admit failure, being honest with yourself, or any of many other possibilities that you, no doubt, understand. True reconciliation requires honesty by both parties—both in the environment leading to it and in the reconciled relationship.

And if you are communicating, demonstrate humility rather than false pride or arrogance. As matters currently exist, a power imbalance between the two of you probably exists or is perceived by your loved one. You are free and can do what you wish—or at least that is the way he sees it. He is locked up, and feels there is little he can do about anything. Therefore, make a special effort to be humble, not just in the sense of being gentle or meek, but also in the sense of being vulnerable and willing take some risks in developing or improving a relationship.

Seeking Reconciliation

Assuming reconciliation is your goal, how do you go about it? Each effort will be different and call for different actions. The following, however, are some guidelines that apply in most situations:

- Put your past behind you and start from where you are—whether you don't have a relationship at all, or have a bad one that needs improving. You cannot create a better past. Move forward.
- Accept your loved one as he is. Remember that you are trying to fix a relationship, not the other person. He may change, but if so, he has to change himself. You cannot do it for him. If he does change, your relationship can change along with him.
- Consider talking about talking. Make a contact—written or verbal—and ask your loved one whether meaningful reconciliation is possible and should even be discussed. You may find it helpful to send a letter suggesting that the two of you simply agree to communicate and try to resolve any issues between you later. Agree to discuss your differences and problems before you start to discuss them.
- Engage in dialogue and tell and listen to your stories. Be sure each of you understands the other's situation, concerns, beliefs, and such. Don't rehash the past as a way of casting blame, but discuss it as a way of understanding one another's humanity and preparing a path for the future.
- Go slow. Surprisingly, you often need to go slow in order to move fast toward reconciliation. Both of you may need time to think about what is happening, adjust to changes, overlook some small issues, accept some disappointments. Taking your time, taking one small step at a time, may be necessary in a reconciliation journey. Celebrate your small successes.

- Don't give up too quickly. It may at first seem that a mutually satisfying relationship is just not possible. Think about the situation and judge the real meaning of what you are hearing and feeling. Each of you may just need time to think and adjust to new possibilities.
- Listen with empathy. To form a healthy, mutually advantageous relationship, the two of you need to understand one another's needs, feelings, and emotions. Listening with empathy and walking in his shoes will allow you to understand him better and will encourage him to listen to you.
- Validate your loved one. Acknowledge his humanity and value as a fellow human being. Regardless of the conflict, you can always find something positive to say. Say it.
- Address your own responsibility and accountability. If you have been wrong (and we are rarely perfect), confess and repent with a sincere apology. Honestly acknowledging your own mistakes is a sign of your strength and maturity, and will set the stage for candid discussions.

Reconciliation may not lead to a perfect relationship. However, trying to reconcile will nearly always bring you and your loved one more peace and start a better chapter in your relationship. That makes it worth the effort.

THINGS TO THINK ABOUT

1. ARE YOU AND _____ ESTRANGED? IF SO, WHY AND FOR HOW LONG?

2. DO EITHER OR BOTH OF YOU ENGAGE IN ANY OF THE FOLLOWING? CHECK THE ONES THAT APPLY.
   ___ PLACE CONDITIONS ON YOUR LOVE.
   ___ ARE NOT OPEN AND HONEST.
   ___ ENGAGE IN EMOTIONAL ABUSE.
   ___ ATTEMPT TO USE COERCION AND THREATS.
   ___ MINIMIZE, DENYY, AND/OR BLAME.
   ___ USE FAMILY AND LOVED ONES.
   ___ DISPLAY RESENTMENT, NOT FORGIVENESS.
   ___ BUILD YOUR RELATIONSHIP ON FANTASY.

3. DESCRIBE THE KIND OF RELATIONSHIP YOU WOULD LIKE TO HAVE WITH _____, AND THE KIND HE WOULD LIKE TO HAVE WITH YOU.

4. WHAT IS THE MOST IMPORTANT THING YOU CAN DO TO CREATE AN ENVIRONMENT THAT WILL LEAD TO A RELATIONSHIP THAT IS AS MUTUALLY SATISFYING AS FEASIBLE UNDER THE CIRCUMSTANCES?

5. LIST THE FIRST THREE THINGS YOU WILL DO TO DEVELOP THIS RELATIONSHIP, AND WHEN YOU WILL DO EACH OF THEM.

12

RESTITUTION

"How can I make amends when I don't even know all those I've hurt?"

Late in 1942, after a series of defeats in World War II, the allies had a remarkable victory in what came to be called the Battle of Egypt. In describing that victory and the hoped for future, British Prime Minister Winston Churchill said, "Now this is not the end. It is not even the beginning of the end. But it is, perhaps, the end of the beginning."

Churchill's phrase aptly describes the situation when your loved one is released from prison. It is not the end of his difficulties. It is probably not even the beginning of the end of his challenges. Life will still be tough after he walks out the prison door. He had problems to start with, and prison may have afforded him additional training in the criminal lifestyle and done little to prepare him for the free world.

He will also be facing what has been described as a "period of invisible punishment," when society will still have its boot on his neck. Finally, he will have a period of "release shock" where the world and life seems surreal to him. Daily tasks you have taken for granted, like driving to the store, making a purchase, setting a regular internal clock with 8 hours of restful sleep, or prioritizing time all seem to overwhelm him. Being pushed to do what seems ordinary to you can make him angry or cause him to withdraw as he feels out of place. Living a successful, law-abiding life will be extraordinarily difficult, and there is a risk he will return through the revolving prison door.

But hopefully your loved one's release is the end of the beginning—the end of the incarceration in which his change began—that will carry him on a continuing journey of transformation to a law-abiding, productive member of society. This brings us to the subject of "restitution."

Restitution involves making amends for the harm one has done. We often think of it as payment, perhaps court-ordered, of compensation by an offender to the victim of his crime for injuries suffered as a result of a criminal act. For example, an offender might pay restitution for his victim's medical bills, lost wages, or damaged property. But this type of restitution is not always possible or practicable. Sometimes the victim is unknown or wants no contact with the perpetrator, sometimes there are too many victims to consider, and sometimes the victim is society at large—involving issues such as increased insurance costs, higher taxes to pay for the criminal justice system, the general degradation of culture, and such.

Symbolic restitution may be appropriate when restitution to the actual victim is not feasible. For example, one convicted of a drug offense might pay for a drug education program, or an offender who assaulted an elderly couple might help make improvements at a local nursing home. Or he might perform a specified number of hours of work for a local government or nonprofit agency.

Even this type of restitution is not always feasible for an offender. Opportunities to pay back for her crime, even symbolically, are limited while she is locked up. And even after release from prison, she is likely to have few if any resources. Meeting parole obligations, making enough money to scrape by, and avoiding another term in prison may be all she can handle.

The fact that society is a victim of all crime allows an offender to make a form of restitution by restoring his life and becoming a good, law-abiding, tax-paying citizen: one who pays back to society rather than drags it down. One who is at the end of the beginning of a new life and is on the threshold of continuing contribution to society. That's the way we will consider it here.

This leads to the issue of what you can do to help your loved one become a productive, law-abiding citizen after release, who continues to succeed rather than return to prison for more time. Start by doing your best to understand the person who is returning.

UNDERSTANDING YOUR LOVED ONE AFTER PRISON

Some people—and some offenders—never learn.

"When I left prison I planned to do the same things I did which was basically smoking weed, working, looking for sex. My attitude was so bad that one friend told me while we were hanging out, 'Richie, you havn't changed.' I responded with, 'Was I suppose to?'"

Don't expect the same person who went to prison to return. Prisons change people. Sometimes their criminal habits become more ingrained. Sometimes they improve their lives. Hopefully your loved one has mainly changed for the better and is living a restored life, perhaps with help from prison rehabilitation programs and your efforts. But, at best, your loved one will have to deal with a number of difficult problems after his release. The following list, borrowed from *The Unvarnished Truth about the Prison Family Journey* by Carolyn Esparaza and Phillip Yow, which they borrowed from the Boston College School of Theology and Ministry, gives a sobering but unfortunately realistic picture of what to expect with recently released offenders. They are likely to exhibit some or many of the following characteristics:

1. Post-release shock and disorientation (no fixed bearings)
2. Lack of continuity/follow through (flaky behavior)
3. Suppressed hostility (seething rage and undifferentiated hate)
4. Lethargy: often extreme social withdrawal and psychological denial
5. Deep-based depression (frequently chronic) resulting in mal-adaptive behavior

6. Financially destitute with a growing sense of anxiety and desperation
7. False expectations and illusions on a multitude of personal and social levels
8. Intense range of fears: personal failure, social and vocational rejections, etc.
9. Severe alienation (man from Mars); often intense, long-term social isolation
10. Cultural shock: cannot relate or adapt to social change and new tempo of life
11. Poor to non-existent problem solving and conflict resolution skills
12. Engulfed in the prison value system: kindness is weakness
13. Personal and cultural inferiority complex ("branded and banished")
14. Compulsive neurotic behavior; minimal stability (addictive mentality)
15. Hunger for instant gratification: "All I want is EVERYTHING NOW."
16. Poor self-esteem/hungry for approval (often actively resistant to disapproval)
17. Compulsive drive to "catch up and catch back:" extreme impatience
18. Confused and frustrated sexual roles, values, and identities
19. Emotionally and perceptually distorted view of self and others
20. Limited employment related skills and out of touch with current market needs
21. Frequently displaying self-destructive attitudes and actions ("bad attitude")
22. A fragile and vulnerable grip on life itself

Obviously, the extent to which each person exhibits these characteristics will vary, depending on the individual, the length and type of incarceration, rehabilitation efforts, and other such factors. But you can expect your loved one to exhibit some or many of them if he has been incarcerated for a significant time. And you need to consider them as you think about what you can do after his release to help him attain an acceptable, productive life—and pay restitution to society.

HELPING YOUR LOVED ONE AFTER PRISON

Once again—your loved one is responsible for his own life, and only he can become a productive, law-abiding citizen and continue to succeed rather than return to prison for more time. But he will face some large challenges, and will probably need your help.

"I am 44 years old. Am a mechanic and have need of everything, a job, Place to live, or Parole too. Cloths, [undecipherable] to get by with until such time as I can secure work in the world."

Consider the following:

Have Realistic Expectations

The person you knew before prison is not the one who will return. The person you think you know in prison is not the one who will return. He has changed, in ways you don't know about and will have great difficulty understanding. Remember that your loved one has been used to a structured, controlled, slower life, where necessities have generally been provided and he was allowed to make few decisions. He has had to suppress his feelings. He felt he couldn't trust anyone. He has had no significant exposure to the opposite sex or to meaningful relationships. He may have lived in fear, or filled with hate and rage. He may be consumed by criminal thinking (see Chapter 5). Your loved almost surely has formed habits that don't work in the free world, and that are very difficult to change.

Consider what is realistic for you to expect from your loved one. If your expectations are too low, you'll fail to acknowledge his abilities and make it seem okay for him to fail. On the other hand, if your expectations are too high, then reality will suffer from comparison to your expectations, and you will see him as a failure, which may cause him to see himself the same way. Some ideas for setting reasonable expectations are:

- Understand what expectations he has for himself. He is unlikely to exceed his own expectations. If your expectations of him are higher than his own, you are likely to be disappointed. To understand his expectations, listen. Ask appropriate questions. Be careful with your advice. Even simple statements like "I believe in you" can feel like pressure. Challenge him to be all he can be without setting him up for failure.

> *"Sis., I sit in my little cubicle most nights wondering if, I am truely ready to be released. I have this vision of the things I want to do. Even though I am getting my AS in culinary arts. I am scared that things will not go right for me. I do not think that things are going to be easy at all. I am a realist."*

- Recognize his limitations as well as his strengths. People often fail because of their limitations or problems, not because they are not trying. Review the list of characteristics in the previous section and consider which may apply to him and cause him problems.
- Think in terms of what he needs rather than what you think he "should do." You cannot control him or make him do what you wish. You can help him meet his basic needs, and this may be all that can be reasonably expected at the time.
- Encourage him to develop a written plan. A plan is fundamentally an organized listing of expectations and how they will be accomplished. Writing one down will help him

be calm and think deeply about what he can and cannot realistically accomplish and how to go about it. (Review Chapter 2 for more thoughts on developing a plan.)
- Be tolerant of his failures and acknowledge his successes. Life after a time of incarceration is difficult. Expect mistakes and failures, and be willing to adjust your expectations downward if necessary. But also acknowledge his successes, however small, help him build on them, and adjust your expectations upward if feasible.
- If your loved one is staying with you, realize that in some ways you have taken on the role of transitional housing for him. Have some reasonable expectations of him. Allowing him to "use" you because you are family may have to be addressed. Remind him that you are happy to be able to help but that some reasonable expectations such as doing laundry, helping with dishes or the yard, etc. would also help you. This lets him know he is of value to you and gives him a boost of self-esteem. He's looking for approval anywhere he can get it and its best if it comes from honest achievement.

"More than anything sis., I am going to need you all to have patience with me. I am also going to need the support of my family. I understand all too well how far behind in life I am."

Encourage Your Loved One to Take First Things First

When your loved one is released, he will be much like a fledgling bird in a nest. If he spreads his wings too soon or too fast and falls out of the nest, something will eat him. He'll go back to prison. He will have many immediate, pressing needs: needs that you may take for granted but that for him can be monumental. He may need to meet with his parole officer and comply with all of her requirements. He will need identification, typically access to a social security card and drivers license; a place to stay; clothing and food; transportation; enough cash to scrape by; medical care, which may require obtaining his prison medical records; and all the many requirements of daily living that he hasn't needed or were provided while he was locked up. And he'll be operating in a world he doesn't know, frequently requiring skills he doesn't have.

"I don't know what I'm going to do for work or anything when I get out. I want to go to school, but I don't know. I'm scared dude. No one knows it, but that's the truth."

If he is living with you, the situation becomes more complex. Your daily challenges will continue, and are likely to grow for a time as strangers try to integrate into one home. Each of you has changed during the incarceration. Both need to acknowledge the changes and accept the fact that things will not be the same as they were before. Focus on the daily routine of life, communicate, and learn to live together.

Encourage your loved one to set written priorities and goals (or—again—develop a plan, as discussed above) to help in dealing with the many new, difficult situations he will face. Work with him on the goals if he is willing. Encourage him to consider three types:

- Short-term priorities for coping in the next few days and weeks: a place to live, food to eat, transportation, assistance in meeting parole requirements, etc.

"I am in need of help! Can you ... help me? If so how? I need a place to parole too."

- Enabling goals: shorter term goals that will enable him to avoid a return to prison and help him attain longer term success: a decent job, some trade school courses, AA meetings, Celebrate Recovery meetings, etc.
- Long-term goals: the kind of life he would like to have in the future: aspirational, over-arching, long-term objectives that he will strive for.

Once he has a plan, your loved one needs to focus initially on one thing at a time—starting with the greatest need. When one is complete, he can check it off and move to the next. After all his immediate needs are met, then he can start working on his enabling goals.

Help your Loved One Find the Right Environment

Research points to a powerful connection between living in an area where there are high levels of poverty, drug use, and crime—and involvement in serious crime. Those who associate with people who are on the margins of society and commit crimes are more likely to commit crimes themselves.

Your incarcerated loved one probably associated with unsavory characters and learned from them before he was locked up. His environment—where he lived and who he associated with—probably influenced him in his criminal activity. If he returns to the same circumstances, he is likely to revert to his old habits and criminal activity.

"Then there is always my 'friends' who will come by looking to do business & want to stay a while to 'help out' when they really just want get as much as he can ..."

You may not be able to do much about where your loved one stays after release. You may yourself live in a high crime area, not because you choose to but because that is all you can afford or for other legitimate reasons. And your loved one is likely to locate near you. But if you have a reasonable choice, don't provide him an incentive to live in an area conducive to crime.

More opportunities may exist to influence who your loved one associates with. First, look in the mirror. Is his association with you positive rather than negative? Does your life pull him down or build him up, set the wrong or right example? For example, was abuse of alcohol a factor in his criminal activity? Does he need to refrain from alcohol use? Do you use alcohol?

How do you think that affects him? Do you need to change who you are as the first step in helping him change who he associates with?

You cannot prevent your loved one from associating with who he wants to, and ragging on him about his poor choice of friends is likely to backfire. But you can present him some options that will help him make better choices about who he hangs with. Spend more time with him. Include him in family events. Invite him to church. Encourage him to enroll in a course and help him do so. Introduce him to people. Help him find things to fill his time—like school or a job. Help him meet his parole conditions so he doesn't call on one of his old—perhaps unsavory—friends for help.

"I am fixing to see parole. And need a better place to parole my mom passed away [recently] and I started getting letters from an ex boy friend you see he's still doing bad things & I dont want that kind of life."

Help Your Loved One Meet His Parole/Probation Obligations

Parole conditions vary from state to state, and sometimes on the basis of the offense for which an offender is convicted. Common provisions include:

- Reporting to his parole officer within a specified time after release
- Staying within a specified area and keeping his parole officer advised of where he is living and working
- Advising his parole officer in advance of any changes in residence, workplace, or travel outside the specified area
- Not possessing firearms, knives, or other weapons
- Not associating with certain individuals, such as persons on parole or probation, inmates in a penitentiary, or gang members

- Not possessing illegal drugs or drug paraphernalia and being subject to drug testing
- Refraining from drinking alcohol
- Participating in mental health or substance abuse treatment
- Finding and maintaining employment
- Submitting to electronic monitoring
- Residence, property, and person being subject to search at any time without notice
- Advising his parole officer if he is arrested or gets a ticket
- Submitting a monthly written report
- Paying a periodic supervision fee
- Meeting special requirements for sex offenders
- Obeying other requirements established by his parole officer, such as cognitive education classes, drug offense classes, DUI classes, and other regular meetings including AA, CA, NA, and others.

If conditions are violated, parole may be revoked and the offender ordered back to prison. Violation may be for committing a new crime, or for breaking the terms of parole, called a "technical" violation. Breaking curfew, or failing to meet with a parole officer, or failing to pass a drug test are examples of technical parole violations. Offenders usually are not sent back to prison for one technical violation. They often are given a second chance, but the "straw that breaks the camel's back" will send them back to the big-house.

Your best opportunities to help your loved one avoid parole violations may well be to help him avoid technical violations: the "easy" things that may result from negligence or from his not having some of the basic necessities for compliance. Think of what he needs in order to comply, and help him get them. For example:
- Adequate transportation to meet with his parole officer
- Involvement in alcohol or drug rehabilitation

> *"I know that drugs and other substance played its role destroying what we had I pray to God that He will never allow me to indulge or put anything that would violate my parole or inter sprits. I have come to realize that we all need some help and support that means a lot to a person that has had addictions for most of his or her life."*

- Sufficient cash to pay parole fees and to "get by"
- Socialization that does not include prohibited people
- An alarm clock or a friendly call to be sure he attends required meetings
- A good listener to help him think through the issues he will be facing
- A cell phone
- A decent job

Help Your Loved One Find Work

Finding employment will be extraordinarily difficult when your loved one is released. He has been out of the work force for some time, probably has no references, and his job skills may be marginal or non-existent. He is likely suffering from cultural shock and may be suffering from low self-esteem. Employers may have a bias against hiring felons, and may bar him from consideration on the basis of a conviction-based disqualification, justified by "business necessity." More importantly, he will face a number of statutes that authorize agencies to suspend or revoke a dizzying array of licenses or permits based on conviction of a felony.

> *"When I do get out. After I report, I am going to go get my AD. Then I am going to take the little money I have and buy some chicken and other food products. I am going to make and sell breakfast tacos. When I get enough money from doing that I will expand a little into other types of food. When I am not selling tacos. I will be looking for a*

job. If it takes me a while to get a job, I will continue to hustle the tacos. If I have not gotten a job in two months, I will build me a BBQ pit."

In this difficult situation, your loved one will need all the help he can get to find work. Some things you can do include:

- Educate him about "the job of getting a job." Buy a good, simple book on looking for work and give it to him. Help him develop a list of daily things to do, a resume, and a model application letter. Teach him minimal computer skills.
- Help him obtain access to the resources needed for a job search: e.g., a telephone, computer, writing material, transportation, etc.
- Use your contacts if you have any. Many, if not most, jobs are obtained through relationships. He probably has few that are positive. If you have any contacts, make introductions and otherwise explore any possibilities you are aware of.
- Help him create an employer friendly email address. He may have used email before but probably for personal reasons. His email address of toughdude@yahoo.com is not going to be well received by an employer. He needs an email address for many applications and job search sites and his email address will matter.
- Help him contact one of many organizations that help felons get jobs, most of which have information available on-line. This may require teaching him the necessary search techniques, assisting with the initial searches, and helping him get signed up when an appropriate organization is found.
- Serve as a mentor. Your loved one may have never held a meaningful job and may not have had a meaningful work experience while in prison. Thus, he may need help in understanding his responsibility as an employee, and what

an employer will expect of him: things as simple as showing up on time, giving a day's work for a day's pay, and finding value in the low wage he may be receiving.
- Continually build him up. He will need the kind of positive reinforcement that only a close friend or family member can provide.

Stick With Your Loved One

Even with a job and both of your best efforts, your loved one's life after release will be difficult—a struggle that seems to have no end. Both of you will have to approach it with persistence and view it, not as an event, but as a journey.

THINGS TO THINK ABOUT

1. HOW HAS _____ CHANGED WHILE HE WAS INCARCERATED?

2. WHAT CAN YOU DO TO MAKE SURE _____ HAS A GOOD LIVING ENVIRONMENT UPON HIS RELEASE?

3. WHAT ARE THE THREE BIGGEST PROBLEMS YOUR LOVED ONE WILL FACE IN THE FREE WORLD?

4. WHAT WILL YOU DO TO HELP HIM WITH EACH OF THESE PROBLEMS?

13

THE JOURNEY

"It will give me important tools to use but only God and myself can truly be responsible for my life."

Think of a hurricane that started as an area of low pressure and slowly swirling winds far out in the ocean, became larger and stronger as it moved toward land, and developed into a fearful, destructive force when it hit the shore. Similarly, most of the problems your loved one is facing started small, grew over time, and became complex, messy situations that are difficult to resolve. Just as they didn't occur overnight, they cannot be resolved overnight. Solving your loved one's problems and conflicts, and restoring peace in his life, requires him to take a journey that lasts a life-time. And to optimize his chance of success, you need to take that long journey with him.

The journey will not be easy or straightforward for either of you. Perhaps your loved one will be locked up for a long time. He may have to deal with the pain of growing old behind bars. You may have to face the sadness of seeing him do so. Even if not, the effects of his lifestyle and his felony conviction will continue well beyond prison. His release will be just a transition from one difficult reality to another. Dealing with drug or alcohol problems may be a lifetime effort. He may have failed to get an education and missed the most productive years of his life. Just getting by financially will be a struggle. He may have no choice but to live in an environment that is conducive to crime. He may have few meaningful relationships, as loved ones and friends from his past have moved on or passed away.

It's important for you to avoid being one of those who moves on. It's critical for you to stick with him, through the good and the bad. Remember the themes that were introduced in Chapter 1:

- You cannot control your loved one or force her to do anything. But you can nurture her and help her succeed.
- Look at yourself, and be a positive role model.
- Your loved one is responsible for her own actions.
- Look to your faith for help and encourage him in his.
- Listen effectively to tell your loved one you care and to gain information you can use in helping with him.

And most important, always love him or her. Remember the words of 1 Corinthians 13:13: "And now these three remain: faith, hope and love. But the greatest of these is love."

Made in the USA
Coppell, TX
01 February 2025